P9-ECN-815

Image
Consulting

The New Career

Joan Timberlake

ACROPOLIS BOOKS LTD.

WASHINGTON, D.C.

ACROPOLIS BOOKS, LTD.
Colortone Building, 2400 17th St., N.W.,
Washington, D.C. 20009

Printed in the United States of America by
COLORTONE PRESS
Creative Graphics, Inc.
Washington, D.C. 20009

Attention: Schools and Corporations
ACROPOLIS books are available at quantity discounts with
bulk purchase for educational, business, or sales promotional
use. For information, please write to: SPECIAL SALES
DEPARTMENT, ACROPOLIS BOOKS LTD., 2400 17th
ST., N.W., WASHINGTON, D.C. 20009

**Are there Acropolis Books you want but cannot find in your
local stores?**
You can get any Acropolis book title in print. Simply send
title and retail price, plus 50 cents per copy to cover mailing
and handling costs for each book desired. District of Columbia residents add applicable sales tax. Enclose check or money
order only, no cash please, to:
ACROPOLIS BOOKS LTD., 2400 17th St., N.W.,
WASHINGTON, D.C. 20009.

Library of Congress Cataloging in Publication Data

Timberlake, Joan,
   Image consulting.

   Includes bibliographical references and index.
   1. Public relations — Vocational guidance.
2. Publicity.   I. Title.
HM263.T54   1983   659.2′023   83-15612
ISBN 0-87491-728-X (pbk.)

Art director: Robert Hickey

To The Image Makers

. . . and, in particular, to my family, friends, and associates who've been an inspiration through the years. An acknowledgment, also, to the special people at Acropolis and their wizardry in helping individuals achieve their dreams, with an extra "thank you" to Kathleen Hughes whose idea was the "launching pad" for this book.

Contents

Introduction

Does this sound like you?

"I enjoyed my career, but wasn't sorry to quit when we had our first child. Now both the first *and* the second are well along in school . . . and I have the time for myself I'd almost forgotten about during their pre-school years!

I could take classes or brush up on skills to return to the kind of job I had before, but I'd like to do something different. I'd want it to be something I'd really enjoy, something that would be useful to others . . . and a career I could arrange to fit my family's schedule.

Or this?

"After graduating as a history major, my mailbox didn't overflow with job offers so when the store where I'd worked during the summer offered me a full-time job, I took it. Now I've discovered I love fashion and want to do more with it!"

Or this?

"I've taught kindergarten for five years . . . am still crazy about kids, but would like to work with color effects more subtle than crayons or fingerpaint pictures!"

Or?

"Desk jobs are okay, but I want to be more than a secretary. People ask my opinion about clothes so often I think I might have a future in fashion.

Many considering a career change into this very special field often think:

"I've been reading so much about image consultants . . . people who recommend colors by special palettes, or those who help others develop the kind of wardrobes that are great image-makers. It all sounds interesting to me, but I'd like to know more about the way these careers really work before I decide to become involved."

Although the idea of a career as an image consultant is a fairly recent development, it is mushrooming. You'll find consultants in small towns as well as large cities. The opportunities are there for creative, marketing-oriented people who like the idea of working with a flexible schedule.

Since we're all judged by others' perceptions of us, we want that crucial first impression to be favorable, whether it's a job interview or a personal encounter. And wearing the right type of fashion, the right colors — achieving the right "total effect" — can help make it happen for anyone!

Introduction

That's why "image" has become the big catchword of the 80's. There is a growing market for advisors who can enhance favorable qualities and make sure that visual communications carry the message the individual wants to create. When you feel good, when you know that what you're wearing is becoming and in the right colors to create a "happy environment," you're bound to be more confident.

Ten or fifteen years ago, those who thought about image were likely to be politicians or part of the entertainment world. Today this has changed dramatically. No longer is it "just for celebrities"!

Who has image consultations done these days? On-target careerists (both men and women) who find that it is a "good buy" for them in terms of creating an image that helps them relate better to their public, and to the decision-makers who affect their professional recognition; women re-entering the job market who want their look to reflect their talent; and harried housewives who've learned they can save time and money by knowing how to target choices that maximize their fashion budget. Many parents even bring their young children along to give them an early start at discovering the colors that show them at their best!

Many of today's image consultants are becoming celebrities themselves. Some win local recognition; others receive national attention. First came John Molloy of *Dress for Success* fame. Then Emily Cho challenged him in *Looking Terrific.* Carole Jackson made color analysis famous with *Color Me Beautiful.* Now Leatrice Eiseman is making headlines by extending personal colortimes into the world around us in *Alive with Color!*

PART I

You, The Image Consultant

Chapter 1

What Is an Image Consultant?

Why They Are in Demand

People like to see themselves in certain ways: bright, attractive, promotion-material, good person to represent the company, power exec, fashion trendsetter (maybe even sexy, but that preference is personal, not boardroom). Because visual and verbal clues add up to a kind of first-impression shorthand, in which few people are fluent, image consultants are providing assistance . . . and making big changes in buying patterns.

As one consultant told us, "There are still a few stores that think we're a flash-in-the-pan idea that's a mere fad, and we'll go away. We won't. In a few years buying patterns will change even more than they have in the last five."

An example of this is the way that women and men today — particularly in the business world — have the desire for power dressing that expresses their own individuality. In the 1970's, these same people were locked into the fear that if they didn't religiously follow a single rule of "success dressing," they'd be doomed to eternal failure!

Today we've gone far beyond such simplistic concepts. *Don't* wear a color if it makes you look terrible! So that suit *is* "rich looking"; if the proportions are wrong for *you*, it's a poor buy! "Mr. Jones *always* pauses before the company's name whenever he gives a speech . . . perhaps I should too!" *Wrong!* Don't blindly copy. *Make the best of your own style* by consulting advisors who know the essence of what's happening in the 80's.

The Colorful Consumer: A Force to Reckon With

The individual who *knows her colors* is becoming a consumer force to reckon with in sales figures since the bottom line *does* make a difference in merchandise availability. This is true far beyond the small boutique. Color-based concepts are surfacing in many places and markets, from department store fashion promotions to in-home direct selling of cosmetics.

While none of three major direct selling companies emphasizes a single special color concept, all are very aware of what color can do. Mary Kay Cosmetics, for example, stresses the importance of coordinating skin-tone depth and intensity with eye shadow, blusher, and lip color. They believe that women have a possible range of colors, and are currently developing a color selector to make their selections easier.

A spokesperson for Avon says that the idea of *the whole image* is "taking the country by storm." Because Avon recognizes that color is the key to makeup sales, they have developed their "Personal Color Harmony." It coordinates makeup colors with wardrobe and skin tones to help their customers achieve a flattering, individual look.

Although Amway's corporate headquarters takes no "color position," they do provide distributors with "color coordinator" information that designates selections as blue-based or yellow-based. Since their representatives have a great deal of independence, a number of them are delving more deeply into the idea of special color cueing, some by taking special training courses and others by doing intensive reading.

When Bloomingdale's announced seasonally oriented shows, each time the demand for reservations was so tremendous that they had to turn down requests at both of their Washington, D.C.-area stores. The nationwide chain of J.C. Penney stores has embarked on a color-analysis program. **Amelia Myers,** Alexandria, Virginia-based merchandise publicity coordinator, credits her counterpart in Atlanta, **Carol Luedecke,** as being the first to bring a color consultant into Penney stores to develop a lecture/color course.

"It's gone from one J.C. Penney market to another. We started preparing for an April promotion very early in the winter . . . to make sure that all of our associates had the information about 'Color Me Beautiful' principles. Their people came in and worked with our merchandisers, then provided more intensified training for the cosmetics associates."

"After all the associates were thoroughly familiar with this way of fashion shopping, we scheduled lectures for the general public. In each store, the response to this was so fantastic that we had to schedule three to seven follow-up classes."

"It's really very exciting to see the results. People feel confident, and the sales associates know exactly how to direct these customers to their colors for fashions that really flatter. I've also noticed that the associates are wearing 'their' colors too!"

Image
Consulting

Looking at the changing color picture from another fashion viewpoint is **Jane Ann Simpson.** She's had a variety of buying assignments with Garfinckel's, a large Washington, D.C. speciality store, including designer sportswear, fine jewelry, and merchandise for the import boutique, and now manages a major suburban branch. "Color consultants are a great idea. Many people in fashion are so accustomed to working with colors and fashion that they may not realize the dilemma that faces a number of individuals. Once the consultant has advised on the right formula of 'colors that are good for you,' it becomes a great time saver, and helps the busy woman or man to shop more quickly and efficiently for their best effects."

Image and Business Success

In *The Extra Edge: Success Strategies for Women (Acropolis Books Ltd., 1983)* authors **Charlene Mitchell** and **Thomas Burdick** survey recent female graduates of the Harvard Business School, who were asked, "How important has your 'image' been in your career progress to date?" Seventy-five percent of those interviewed said that "image" was an important or very important factor in their success "and would continue to be even at top management levels."

In pointing out that "image" is the sum total of the parts an individual presents to the world, and that what's good for one industry may not be for another, they note that individuality and the ability to attract attention favorably are distinct advantages in the climb to the top.

Harvard career counselor **Kathy Fox**, who advises middle-management women, says: "It's vital to a woman's success to express her individuality. When she stops imitating her peers and makes that psychological 'jump' into her own true identity, her career enters a new, more successful phase."

Color, Fashion, and the Public Image Consultant

No wonder image consulting has become a hot new career option! Although there are many who consider themselves involved in this field (a banker could be a financial image consultant or a caterer an entertaining specialist), *Image Consulting* concentrates on three personal elements: *Color, Fashion, and Public Image.*

"In the past few years there have been tremendous changes in the field of image," says **Brenda York** of York & Associates. "Today corporations and human resources or training areas are far more receptive to the idea of seminars. Also, the biggest new single market is now the 'baby boom' men who are approaching 40. Many never had anyone to train them in what looks good on them, but they are part of a generation that strives to compete successfully. They realize that if they haven't learned in the past, it is important they they know *now* . . . especially in a tight job market. One has to be much sharper today to really make it on the first impression."

The Color Consultants — Who are They?

Many color consultants started out with little more than an interest in color and fashion, but, after studying and special training, have become experts in advising people about their most flattering colors. Their expertise gives them the confidence to make helpful recommendations. It's important to work with a system in which you totally believe — whether it's based on the four seasons, or the sunrise to sunset principle, or on a similar concept built on color harmonies. Because of the overlap between color and the fashion world, many color consultants find themselves offering fashion and makeup advice to their clients.

The Fashion Consultant

Who are the Fashion Consultants? They know that a love of shopping does not equal instant fashion advisor! Fashion consultants may have had store selling experience or seen the business from the wholesale angle, but they're definitely "clothes-wise" people with a keen sense of fit, proportion, and what's appropriate for which occasion. Their clients depend on their flair for coming up with the clothes they need as "image builders."

The Public Image Consultant

Public image consultants help clients overcome nervousness or anxieties that may prevent them from being at their best in public. They assist in speech-writing and delivery style, show their clients how to deal with the media, reinforce their aura of success, and can actually change public opinion. Their job is that of a teacher or communicator.

Key Requirement: A Good Eye

There's no single background from which image consultants emerge, so don't fall into the trap of thinking "Oh, she has her doctorate or he's a high-powered fashion consultant to Fortune 500 companies — how can I as an 'Average Joan or Joe' do this!" You *can*. Start right now by using your eyes and ears to be aware of current trends. Even the experts admit that while it's ideal to be born with creative flair, one learns a lot by observing.

Read books that relate to the field, and continue thinking about the information that you acquire; *really* apply it. You may not become an instant expert, but you will be taking a *big step toward your goal*. And the more experience you add, the closer you get!

Some of the characteristics image consultants seem to share are: A good "eye" for color, line, and appropriateness; a feeling for each individual's potential; and a true appreciation of people. They have also learned how to market themselves and their clients astutely, and to understand what appeals to today's public.

Ruthanne Olds, image consultant to larger-sized women, identifies three important credentials:

"As an image consultant you want to get as much exposure as you can, so that you're sure you have the qualifications you need *before* you set yourself up in this field. You need

1. an excellent eye for color,

2. an understanding of the principles of art — and how to apply them to the human body, and

3. a sensitivity to peoples' insecurities."

Keep these needs in mind, but remember one other thing: There are *many* levels of success in this field. You don't have to be a national celebrity to prove it!

A Growth Profession

Image consulting is thriving despite current economic realities. Could it be that people need more "personal P.R." to sell themselves in hard times?!

Andy Warhol has suggested that anyone can be a celebrity for 15 minutes, but most of us are alloted much less time to make an impression. That's why image consulting has become such a booming business . . . with national publications predicting an even brighter future!

William Friend in "Personal Packaging, A Look at the New Image Makers," in the April 1983 issue of *Association Management* magazine, quotes **Barbara Blaes** on the mushrooming growth of the personal image field: "People would be amazed at how much importance associations and major corporations attach to personal appearance. A lot of them say, 'Either you have the right image or it's goodbye.' " She believes that the reason a number of women aren't being listened to or promoted is that they need to realize "you have to look as if you belong in the league before you can be accepted."[1]

The October 1982 issue of *Entrepreneur* Magazine's "Color This Consulting Business Successful" emphasized that "with a little training you can be a consultant who is on top of the latest craze. The secret of your success in this will be your ability to market and to communicate one-on-one."[2]

The Flexible Career

To anyone who was formerly in a job where being one minute late was cause for a frown (or worse!) the freedom as an image consultant is almost unbelievable. You set your own schedule, and are the one to decide *where* you want to work:

- out of your own home

- out of an office,

- by making a "space arrangement" with a store, school, or beauty shop,

- or even working out of a suitcase!

The Low Capital Investment Career

And, for someone just beginning, image consulting has still another "plus." It's the kind of career that can get off the ground with a relatively small investment.

Satisfying as this career is, like any other, it offers challenges as well as opportunities. Any time you decide to become your own boss, there's a great deal you should be aware of when (and before!) you set forth. Let's look at the important essentials to keep in mind.

What You Can Do

1. Develop your eye for color by really observing. See how different people look in the same color, what combinations appear to be most effective.

2. Be aware of how the proper (or improper) proportioning affects not only the piece concerned, but the total look. Study what top executives in your area are wearing, what the stores are offering.

3. Make decisions about the type of image consultancy you think would be a "good fit" for you.

4. Consider how involved you want to become — how many hours you want to work, how much money you need to earn.

Chapter 2

How Do You Fit Into The Picture?

Getting Started

Before you do anything as drastic as giving notice this very moment on your current job, read on!

These special tests will help you target your interests and aptitudes — the combination of qualities that can determine your chances of making it successfully as a consultant-entrepreneur.

Do You Have What It Takes? A Quiz

		TRUE	FALSE
1.	If you were an artist, you would rather be a painter than a sculptor.	___	___
2.	Your family and friends "draft" you to be their personal shopper because they prefer your fashion choices to their own.		

	TRUE	FALSE

3. When entertaining, you believe that it's just as important to create a treat for the eyes as for the taste. _____ _____

4. In order to relax you'd rather take a walk on the beach or in the woods than go to a concert. _____ _____

5. When you decorate, your eye for exact color may cause complications for the painters, but they admit you were right when the job is done. _____ _____

6. You'd like to capitalize on your flair for color and line by making a profession of it. _____ _____

7. Although you are interested in money, accomplishing something useful is a prime factor in your career choices. _____ _____

8. When you make up your mind to do something, you don't just rely on "wishing to make it so," but invest the necessary time, energy, and money to make your determination pay off. _____ _____

9. You prefer the one-on-one involvement of working closely with people to more abstract jobs. _____ _____

10. You have a strong interest in the psychology of color and its effects on human well-being. _____ _____

Did you check mostly "Trues?" You are lucky to have an instinctive gift for color and line; you may already have studied art or worked in merchandising. If you checked mostly "False" answers you might be able to make it as a consultant, but would probably find greater happiness and success in another aspect of this field.

To be an image consultant (or any kind of entrepreneur) you need a good deal of business sense. Some people do very well working for others, but may lack certain essentials to succeed on their own. *Before* you decide to become an entrepreneur, take a realistic look at the kind of person you really are — bring that "floaty" picture of yourself into focus. By doing so, you can avoid a lot of problems. To help provide information about key points, here is a special test prepared by career consultants **Dr. S. Norman Feingold** and **Dr. Leonard G. Perlman.**[3]

Check the answers that fit:

1.   Are you a self-starter?

a. I do things on my own. Nobody has to tell me to get going.

b. If someone gets me started, I keep going all right.

c. Easy does it. I don't put myself out until I have to.

2.   How do you feel about other people?

a. I like people. I can get along with just about anybody.

b. I have plenty of friends — I don't need anyone else.

c. Most people irritate me.

3.   Can you lead others?

a. I can get most people to go along when I start something.

b. I can give the orders if someone tells me what
we should do.   _____

c. I let someone else get things moving. Then I go
along if I feel like it.   _____

4. Can you take responsiblity?

a. I like to take charge of things and see them
through.   _____

b. I'll take over if I have to, but I'd rather let
someone else be responsible.   _____

c. There's always some eager beaver around
waiting to show us how smart he/she is. I say
let him.   _____

5. How good an organizer are you?

a. I like to have a plan before I start. I'm usually
the one to get things lined up when the group
wants to do something.   _____

b. I do all right unless things get too confused.
Then I quit.   _____

c. You get all set and then something comes along
and presents too many problems. So I just take
things as they come.   _____

6. How good a worker are you?

a. I can keep going as long as I need to. I don't
mind working hard for something I want.   _____

b. I'll work hard for a while, but when I've had
   enough; that's it. _____

c. I can't see that hard work gets you anywhere. _____

7. Can you stick with it?

a. If I make up my mind to do something, I don't
   let anything stop me. _____

b. I usually finish what I start — if it goes well. _____

c. If it doesn't go well right away, I quit. Why
   beat your brains out? _____

8. Can you make decisions?

a. I can make up my mind in a hurry if I have to.
   It usually turns out okay, too. _____

b. I can if I have plenty of time. If I have to make
   up my mind fast, I think later I should have
   decided the other way. _____

c. I don't like to be the one who has to decide. _____

9. Can people trust what you say?

a. You bet they can. I don't say things I don't
   mean. _____

b. I try to be on the level most of the time, but
   sometimes I just say what's easiest. _____

c. Why bother if the other person doesn't know the
   difference. _____

10. How good is your health?

a. I never run down! _____

b. I have enough energy for most things I want to
do. _____

c. I run out of energy sooner than most of my
friends seem to. _____

If most of your checks are beside the *first answer*, you probably *have
what it takes* to run a business. If most are by the *second answer*
to each question, you're likely to have more trouble than you can
handle by yourself; you might want to find a partner who is strong
on the points you are weak on. If most checks are beside the *third
answer*, you should reconsider your plans very carefully since you
will probably have an uphill battle ahead of you.

Why? Because initiative, positive attitudes toward others, leadership,
a sense of responsiblity, organization, a strong commitment to work,
industriousness, and adaptability are the keys to success for the independent person.[3] Now that you've "checked out" your success in-
gredients, and determined that you have a fashion "eye" and small-
business personality, what's next?

Visit a variety of stores in your local mall and you'll see!

Start with your own image

Fortunate are those who have a dream or idea, and *instantly set forth*
to turn it into reality! For most of us, the process isn't quite that
simple. In fact, getting started may be the most difficult thing we do.

We fear failure. We're even a little leery of success! We wonder if
that INsecurity blanket we're dragging around might not be big
enough to cover the entire Great Wall of China.

We're definitely not our own best friend when we play non-stop critic as an inner voice utters confidence-destroying thoughts. They pop up faster than bread from the toaster, but the all-time favorite continues to be: "Who do you think you're kidding!" . . . accompanied by remarks like:

- "Why should *anyone* come to Mary Smith for color consultation . . . Mary Smith who flunked finger-painting in the first grade!"

- "Mary Smith — a fashion consultant? What a laugh! Who could forget the first job interview and that outfit that was supposed to be terrific? Tacky-o-la! No wonder the job fell through!"

- "Mary Smith, a public image consultant? Mary Smith, who got stage fright and forgot her single line as the maid in the senior play!"

Don't wallow in inadequacies. That inner voice may be busily dredging up the past's humiliating memories, but you're overlooking something. Mary Smith really has come a long way since then. What about your *accomplishments?* . . . the picture that won a blue ribbon in the areawide art show for its imaginative use of color . . . or the time Mary Smith was asked to coordinate the big charity fashion show because "she always dresses so well" . . . or Mary Smith's testimony at the city council meeting, which convinced the council to install a badly needed traffic light near the school?

We all change and grow as we go through life so let's be as fair to ourselves as we'd be to outsiders . . . give ourselves as much credit as we should. About those liabilities. Don't just accept them — see what's really holding you back and get on with it. Need more training? Get it. Don't have the money? Figure out ways to save or earn extra. Feel overwhelmend? Take it a step at a time. Start small, but *start*.

There is something (I'm the first to admit) about being confronted with a huge list of things to be done, all of which seem to need attention simultaneously. It makes us feel "What's the use?" and can lead to a case of terminal procrastination. Maybe you *can't* work out a complete career plan, but you'd be surprised how much can be accomplished a "nibble" at a time. (There is one good side effect of procrastination — but it's not one that will help you plan a new career. You'll be surprised how often you'll tackle a previously put-off task, simply because it seems less threatening than taking on the unexplored!)

There are lots of ways you can fight procrastination. One of the easiest is to think of yourself as a product — Mary Widget, or whatever you like. Why would you buy this product? What are the benefits to the purchaser? Are there any disadvantages that could be overcome to make the product more salable, and to reach a larger share of the market? How should I price this "product"?

Be honest with yourself. Think about your knowledge and talent. How confident are you that you can convince others of the rightness of your opinions? Perhaps you need to brush up on your skills, or to take some new courses. You may find what's needed right in your local college's free or almost-free continuing education courses, and decide to learn more about art or consider taking courses in textiles or merchandising.

Looking into Professional Training Programs

Check out professional training programs such as those offered by leading color systems or highly skilled consultants. There are also well-known schools such as the Fashion Academy® in Costa Mesa, California, where **Carole Jackson** studied in 1972. Their intensive two-and-one-half week program currently offers a schedule like this:

Week I

1st Friday

Morning — Introduction, distribution of materials
including the 169-page *Your New Image*
(through color & line)
Afternoon — Lecture: "Theory and Principle of Color"
Demonstration of technique

Saturday

All day — Color Enrichment,
draping, and technique

Monday

Morning — Color Enrichment
Afternoon — Color Draping Practice
Evening — "The Color Lecture"

Tuesday

Morning — "The Personality Lecture"
Afternoon — Personality Enrichment
Evening — Hair Seminar

Wednesday

Morning — "The Line Analysis Lecture"
Afternoon — Individual Line Analysis
Evening — "The Line Lecture" and application

Thursday

Morning — "The Accessories Lecture"
Afternoon — "The Wardrobe Lecture"
Evening — Wardrobe Planning Enrichment

Friday

       Morning — Color Technique Enrichment

       Preparations for Saturday

       Afternoon — Color Draping Practice

Saturday

       Morning — Color Draping, Outside Guests

       Afternoon — Color Discussion

Week II

Monday

       Morning — "The Skin Care Lecture"

       Skin Care and Makeup

       Seasonal Concept

       Afternoon — Individual Practice

       Evening — Individual Practice

Tuesday

       Morning — Marketing, P.R., and Bookkeeping

       Afternoon — Fabric, Fiber, and Fashion Lecture

       Evening — Line Enrichment

Wednesday

       All day and evening — Line Practice I, II, III

       Private Consultation and Wardrobe Planning

       Individual Business Consultations

Thursday

       Morning — Eye Makeup Technique

       Color Enrichment

       Afternoon — Color Draping Practice

       Evening — Makeup Enrichment

Friday

       Morning — Final Exam and review

       Afternoon — Graduation

Trying It on a Part-time Basis

Since business experience in any field is useful for consultants who start their own businesses, you may want to test yourself in a different way. For example, if you never have sold before, try working at least part-time in fashion or cosmetics at the best store in your area.

Almost every image person agrees that hands-on experience is invaluable. Anyone who becomes a success in sales learns to get a fairly fast fix on the image the customer wants, what's available, and the best way to bridge the difference between his or her fantasy view and the physical reality.

When you're in and out of a fitting room with a customer, you learn to work closely with that individual . . . or find out quickly if you would rather be doing something else! If so, you've lost very little time, and no money. There's also the possibility that you become so successful as a salesperson that you continue in this capacity rather than become a self-employed advisor.

Read the "help wanted" ads thoroughly if you decide to look for employment first. You will probably see a number of "blind boxes." These are the ones that tell what they're looking for but don't say who they are and list a P.O. box number instead of a name. Most are perfectly legitimate. Some aren't, however, or they glorify the job so much that the current incumbent, if there is one, wouldn't even recognize the job description! Occasionally you see an ad for "Color Consultants," which requests candidates who are "Fashionable. Personable. Professional fashion or makeup background preferred. Will train." Sounds good, but be careful when you respond. If your response results in an interview, check the organization thoroughly to make sure it's responsible, and not a fly-by-night out to get your money. The image-consultant field is booming today and presents both challenges and opportunities.

Positive Pessimism

There are various systems already in use. You may decide after having your colors done that you'd like to become a franchised representative. That's fine if you work it out with the organization, but *don't* decide to go out on your own without this authority and call yourself "Mary Smith's Color Me Beautiful," "Color 1," "Beauty for All Seasons," or some other name or method that is protected by a trademark. This would be infringement and can get you into a legal hassle. Many individual consultants do follow established general principles, but they should never become copycat pirates.

That's my first lesson in "positive pessimism." Thinking of all the things that could possibly go wrong may seem demoralizing, but it's not. If you can get in the habit of thinking about the worst thing that could occur in a variety of situations, and the ways in which you'd cope, you'll be surprised at how much more confident you'll grow.

One organization I worked for had staff-run annual conventions. The planning stage was sometimes chaotic, but when the event actually began, smooth efficiency was the order of the day, thanks to back-up plans for every conceivable contingency. (A minor inconvenience was the impetus for this comprehensive planning — an important speaker had picked up a water pitcher, which was empty!)

You can apply this "looking for trouble" philosophy to your own business. *What if* someone is dissatisfied with her new look? Take extra time to study her *before* you make recommendations. Suggest that she give herself time to become comfortable with the change, and work out a plan with subtle variations that can be used without destroying the total effect. *What if* your clients are satisfied, but no new ones are in sight, and the market seems to be drying up? Broaden your self-marketing. There are lots of people out there who could benefit from your services, but you can't count on them hacking their way through the jungle to find you. Make it easier for them to know about you, and how they can benefit from your image-building. There are lots of ways you can do this without actually advertising.

Some Good Advice

Author and color authority **Leatrice Eiseman** has some practical ideas about what to do when you're getting started:

"Before you go out on your own, it's good to get a job in retailing. By going to the best store in your area and working, even part-time, you have the opportunity to learn about merchandising, display, how to advise people on fashion, color decisions, and possibly interior design."

Eiseman believes that the fledgling consultant should be willing to volunteer her services as a speaker for community groups such as the Welcome Wagon's Newcomers' Club, or consumer education classes. She says, "Share what you know with your community when you address these groups, not only do you give back to the community, you see the ways in which things we give come back to us. Each time you speak you will be establishing your name, and acquiring confidence and experience. Women too often underestimate the volunteer work they've done. Everything taps into what we are."

How much will you charge your paying clients? Outside major metropolitan areas such as New York and Los Angeles, Eiseman says that the basic consulting fee is approximately $35 an hour, but recommends that you check your own area. (The fee she mentions applies to color or fashion consultants, not public image consultants or speech coaches, whose fees for individual instruction might be in the $150-$200 range.)

Color expert Eiseman warns that if you overchange, you'll lose business; if you under-cut, not only will you be unfair to other consultants, but you may be considered a cut-rate product. She also cautions that since clients are paying for your time, make sure you save them money when shopping. She does this by prior "typecasting to store" — analyzing the way the client sees herself and her budget — and, when possible, suggesting shopping malls with many stores to choose from. When seasonal merchandise is not available when needed, she often takes clients to discount centers where such merchandise is available at substantial savings.

Building Your Client List

How do you build your client list — and get repeat business? "Contact *every* civic group, *every* place where women get involved," she advises. "You never know what 'just one more call' may achieve, so don't be shy about it! There are also many opportunities for seminars in industry, but *you* are the person who has to make the opportunity. Check on areas such as 'Women's Asset Committees' and then try to talk them into scheduling one of your seminars. And time it for lunch hour or right at closing to make it easier for people to attend.

"There's one great thing about color/image consulting — it's wonderful to have a career where you can frequently work out of your own home!"

Start With Your Friends

Now that you've thought hard about your new career, done your background reading, had special training if necessary, ordered your stationery and "props," you need *clients*. You've learned how to *build* your list, but how do you get the word out in the first place?

Think of the people who are likely to be your best "press agents" and offer to do their colors, to go shopping with them for special outfits, or to help them prepare for public appearances. (You may want to swear them to secrecy about the fact that you're doing this as a freebie so others won't ask for the same — even if you may be doing some others as well.) A little flattery may get you somewhere if you tell your friend that you've selected her because she is a leader and is considered an opinion-maker. Let her know that you would like her to tell others if she's satisfied, but if she's not, you want to know her reasons so that you will have guidelines for future use.

If other friends feel left out you can always say, "I know how kind you are — you'd say you liked what I did for you even if you didn't. But we all know Joan — if she's not satisfied, she won't hesitate to tell the whole town! Since she *was* pleased, why not have me give a demonstration at the club — and I'll use you as my model!"

It may take a while for your name to catch on, but each time you make a public appearance, be sure that you have your card or brochure available for people to pick up. Get a list of attendees and follow up with a letter . . . possibly offering club members a discount.

Makeup artist **Clare Miller** suggests identifying your "ideal" client market, and thinking of creative ways to bring yourself to the attention of its leadership. Turn key leaders into clients, and your entree is established.

If clients compliment you on what you've done, ask them if you may use them as references. Some will be pleased to have their names used; others may be willing to be quoted as long as it is done "anonymously." If you have to do this, you may want to put the person's occupation or an initial to indicate that you *do* have a variety of people who are clients. Some individuals may cynically believe you've made up such testimonials, but you *do* have real names if questioned, although it's very unlikely that someone would confront you in this way.

It would be great to be the *first* in your area to provide the kind of service you plan to offer. However, don't be discouraged if you're not. What you want to do is to concentrate on what makes *your* approach special . . . then try to get publicity in the local media by emphasizing what's newsworthy about it (in other words, the "U.S.A." — or unique selling angle!) Maybe you specialize in a different type of client. Maybe you have a distinctive background. Maybe you can highlight some unusual or heartwarming experience you've had with a client.

The best thing to do is to sit down and think about yourself as an outsider might. What would be the most interesting or unusual aspect of Mary Smith, image consultant, that you'd like to read, see, or hear about?

What You Can Do

1. Stop procrastinating . . . think of one thing you can do to get you on your way right *now.*

2. Investigate classes . . . continuing education, local schools or other professional development programs.

3. Check out local charges for image consultant assistance.

4. Go to the library or bookstore . . . start your background reading.

5. Make a list of your special strengths which would be valuable as a consultant.

6. Read "help wanted" ads to see what related part-time jobs may be available . . . or call leading area stores.

7. Volunteer to speak before local groups.

8. Look at your own image. Do you look like a "success?"

9. Request a counseling session with your Small Business Administration field office by filling out and sending in the form that follows.

Request Form For Counseling From SBA

NOTE: This form is reproduced in its entirety for your information.

I request appropriate management or technical assistance from the Small Business Administration.

It is understood that such assistance will be provided to me free of charge and that I incur no obligation to reimburse SBA or its counselor(s) providing such assistance.

I authorize SBA to furnish information and data concerning me to the counselor(s) providing such assistance.

I understand that the counselor(s) providing assistance to me have agreed that they will not:

(1) recommend the purchase of goods or services from sources in which he has an interest. or represents, and

(2) accept fees or commissions from third parties who have supplied goods or services to me on their recommendations

This request may be withdrawn at any time upon written notice to SBA unless I am an SBA borrower.

In consideration of the furnishing of management and technical assistance to me, I waive all claims against SBA personnel or counselors arising in connection with this assistance.

Type of Service Requested (Check Appropriate Box)							
	SCORE-ACE		SBI		406		Prof. Assoc.
Complete Below and Sign							
Name of Company						Telephone	
Address (Include ZIP Code)							
Referred to SBA By				Type of Business			
Signature and Title of Company Official						Date	

For addresses and telephone numbers of SBA field offices, look under 'United States Government' in your local telephone directory.

Data To Be Completed By Applicant

For the assignment of a qualified counselor(s), please complete this questionnaire before returning to SBA. Any information given here or during counseling will be held in strictest confidence. (SBA personnel: insert address of your local office below)

As soon as you have completed this form and returned it to the address given above, a counselor will be assigned to you.

I request counseling regarding (check appropriate boxes):

☐ My present business   Year founded _____   ☐ Starting a new   ☐ Sole Proprietorship
☐ Purchasing a business   No. of employees   business   ☐ Partnership
                           _____   ☐ Corporation

Kind of business and goods (or services) offered are as indicated below:

☐ Retail (Selling) _____   ☐ Wholesale (Selling) _____
☐ Service (Kind) _____   ☐ Other (Specify) _____
☐ Manufacturing (Product) _____   Years of experience in
                                                this kind of business _____

Can you furnish a recent balance sheet?   ☐ Yes ☐ No   Have you ever applied for an SBA loan? ☐ Yes ☐ No
Can you furnish a recent profit-and-loss   Do you now have an SBA loan?   ☐ Yes ☐ No
statement?   ☐ Yes ☐ No

Check the problem areas for which you seek counseling

☐ 1. Sales promotion & advertising   ☐ 9. Office & Plant Management
☐ 2. Purchasing   ☐ 10. Government Procurement
☐ 3. Engineering and research   ☐ 11. Merchandising, inventory
☐ 4. Financial analysis   selection & control
☐ 5. Foreign trade   ☐ 12.
☐ 6. Records & Credit Collections   ☐ 13.
☐ 7. Market Research   ☐ 14.
☐ 8. Personnel   ☐ 15. Other

If the following information is available please complete, if not, leave blank.

Employer's ID # (IRS)	Social Security Number	Loan Number

Viet. Veteran ☐ Yes ☐ No	Veteran ☐ Yes ☐ No	Name of County

What in your opinion is the greatest problem in your business operation?

Image
Consulting

43

Chapter 3

Start-up Costs: Time, Money, Paperwork

Time & Money - the Success Twins

We've talked about procrastination. Time authorities often recommend carrying around a small notebook in which you make a daily "to do" list. To make it more useful, assign high, medium, or low priorities to the items. You will then be less likely to spend prime-time hours on personal calls when you should be taking care of high-priority business-getters such as working up a direct mail letter, telephoning prospects, or making a list of potential clients. All of these things do take time but, as color specialist **Leatrice Eiseman** points out, are necessary parts of your time investment. They are also the things that you should *continue* doing on a regular basis even after you are a success. You want to *maintain* visibility, not just to enjoy a brief moment in the spotlight and then blend into the shadows when the next good consultant comes along.

Professional image consultant **James Gray** believes that you should count on five years to build your business to the point where you would consider it a *real* success. Take this into consideration when you start out. Plan on this amount of time and figure out what your financial needs will be, and how to make use of the cyclical ups and downs. Concentrate on ways to map a constant growth pattern, and be sure to keep in touch with your clients. Some may need encouragement to use your service initially, but also you should try to keep in touch with them afterwards to see how they are making use of your advice — to make sure they benefit by applying it. And remember: what you are selling is a service, not a product.

Your Biggest Expenses

Money is that five-letter word we all need for survival. How much money it will take to establish you as an image consultant depends on several things: What level of expertise and visibility are you seeking? How quickly do you want to get established? For example, are you willing to work out of a suitcase or do you want an office of your own from the beginning? How much money do you have budgeted (or can get others to invest) for start-ups and to sustain the business over a certain period of time?

Your biggest expense will probably be the training, which can run from several hundred to several thousand dollars.

Mary Pennisi, a Texas-based color consultant, recalls that she spent about $2,500 for color consultation training, and about $1,000 to get the right balance of fabrics she wanted for the color drapes she felt that she should have. "After that, I really didn't have very much to invest because I started out at home — and there certainly wasn't any overhead there!"

Image consultant **Holly Sallade** found that time was her most costly investment — planning and putting her color program together. Next, in actual dollars came printing, and advertising/marketing of information. "You really must do everything 100 percent — go for the best — and keep improving *always* !"

If you become a makeup consultant, **Clare Miller** recommends that you keep yourself educated on state-of-the-art advances in your field, which includes reading periodicals that pinpoint even fleeting fashion trends. "Taking the time to develop the knowledge that attracts a foundation of happy, enthusiastic clients (whose word-of-mouth advertising brings even more clients) is worth every cent and minute."

When she started out as a fashion consultant, **Cindy Harsley** had to achieve a delicate balancing act of time, organization, logistics, and marketing of her services.

"When I began, my greatest expense was time! I tried to do too much all at once. I was overbooking clients on the same day, dashing around, trying to organize and keep *everything* in order. It took time to accumulate enough clients so that I reached the point of making a living at this career rather than doing it as a sideline or profitable hobby."

The kind of public relations/public affairs consultancy that deals with advocacy issues faces a different kind of challenge, but beginners' needs in time and money are remarkably similar. Californian **Peter Hannaford,** Chairman of the Board of The Hannaford Company, Inc., recalls that when he started his own public relations firm in 1972, "The chief expense was in start-up costs, furniture, equipment, and a little working capital.

"The greatest expense, in terms of time, was in client service and new business development. I'd had a good teacher, my first employer, **Helen Kennedy Rogers.** From her I learned that it was important to learn from mistakes and not to over-promise. I also felt that it was important to be reliable. Do what you say you are going to, so people know that they can count on you."

Additional expenses will depend upon the type of image consultant you plan to become. If color consultants have not received the color materials they need in the classes they've taken, they should count on having enough fabric samples (large enough so that a client can see the color difference, not itsy-bitsy squares that disappear between the fingers) and cosmetics to provide a reality picture for the clients. Color consultants should also have access to a room with white walls to avoid unwanted color reflections. This expense may depend upon the room's availability or the consultant's skill with a paintbrush.

Fashion consultants probably have the lowest initial expense, but they should budget for fashion magazines and specialized papers such as *Women's Wear Daily*, or its more general-interest biweekly sister publication, *W*, to keep up with current and incoming trends. They should also try to get to the really important events in their own area to see which current "in-fashions" look best on real people (and which ones don't quite make it), the particular designers or looks favored by local fashion leaders, and the degree of dressing that's appropriate overall. (You may find a private notebook for your conclusions an especially useful tool.) Be sure to check with your tax person to see how much of this can be considered legitimate business expenses.

The invention of videotaping equipment certainly simplified the public image consultant's advisory role. Tact can go only so far, but when a client sees herself or himself as they actually appear to others, there's no way they can fool themselves about the way their speech or presentation *really* comes across. The client needs to work with a pro for coaching, but videotapes are a very important part of a public image consultant's tools of the trade.

Although this equipment can be so expensive that few fledgling consultants are likely to set up a fully equipped taping studio, you can get around this by making arrangements with organizations that have the equipment. (For starters, check the local Yellow Pages for the listings of video-system distributors or dealers.)

General expenses include stationery and business cards. Don't stint here. There is a big difference between something that is a good value for its price, and a real "cheapie," which looks it! If you let yourself think that a moment's fleeting glance doesn't matter, you'll soon find out that it does! When looking at catalog styles, ask for samples of paper stock before you get too involved. Local printers should have sample books available. Talk with a "pro" — a good printing salesperson or department store stationery advisor — about their recommendations for type faces and the image you want your business papers to project.

Eager as you are to get started, you should have *all* your supplies on hand when you schedule your promotions to make the best impression. Don't use makeshift versions — offered with apologies!

While you are playing this "waiting game," do background reading that relates to your field. It can save you all sorts of pitfalls later, and help you be prepared to handle a variety of situations knowledgably and smoothly.

Boning Up

When **Dr. Deanna Radeloff** was in the early stages of her color consultancy, she read a number of popular books on color, which recalled a text she'd used when she was in college.

"When I looked up **Harriet McJimsey** in our university library, I found that she, along with **Grace Morton,** really had done outstanding academic work on color analysis as far back as 1940. But one of my most interesting research discoveries was the book *Women in America: From Colonial Times to the Twentieth Century*. **Woolson** was the editor and **Robert Brothers of Boston** published it in 1874. Over a century ago this book was predicting the kind of image consultancies we have today as this quote shows:

". . . Then we shall begin to have doctors of dress; and there will be specialists in the profession, those who will recommend to us colors and textures, those who will see to it that we are so well dressed that no one can tell what we wear, and so comfortably attired that self and clothes blend into an harmonious whole."

Who knows what *you* may discover in your own reading! The bibliography in the back of this book lists a number of titles that can answer many different cries for "help!" But for *really* mind-boggling variety, explore the books on color, fashion, public image, and related business topics listed in *Books in Print*, which is available at your local library, or in book stores.

Start-up Paperwork Pandemonium

Starting any kind of business requires a great deal of paperwork, and answers to many questions:

As a sole proprietor, do you know what kind of licenses are required by your city, state, and county?

Will you be prepared for the kind of taxes you must pay — social security, estimated income, possibly personal property on special business equipment (and perhaps withholding taxes when you're successful enough to add employees)?

What kind of insurance should you have — general liability, accident, theft and vandalism, health, or disability protection in case you should be prevented from working?

Are you aware of consumer protection regulations?

Have you determined that there is a sufficient market for your service so that you can make a profit?

Do you know how to set up a record-keeping system? (A simple method many recommend is to purchase the kind of book that makes it easy for you to record all income and expenditures; all office supply stores carry them.)

Don't throw up your hands and say, "But it all seemed *so simple* when I first had my idea of becoming an image consultant. I think I'll give up!" NO, YOU WON'T! You're not alone as "poor, pitiful Pearl". . . there are numerous experts around (free and for fee) who can advise you.

For starters, check *Making It On Your Own* — particularly Chapter Five, "Your Going Concern: Accounting, Taxes, Advertising, Management." In it is a line that could well be a motto for *every* small business person, whether photographer, plumber, or freelancer:

"No matter what kind of business you dream up, it will have to be run as a business if you are going to succeed."

Free Assistance

Authors **Dr. S. Norman Feingold** and **Dr. Leonard G. Perlman,** have a number of recommendations for assistance. One source in particular is geared to women, and offers seminars on subjects like marketing, financing, and overall management techniques. It is the American Women's Economic Development Corporation, 68 E. 42nd St., New York, NY 10165 (212/692-9100).

Another, of course, is the Small Business Administration (SBA), whose regional offices offer all kinds of management assistance — workshops, seminars, films, publications, and training courses. Much of the training is co-sponsored by local civic and business organizations, professional associations, and schools. SBA also provides in-depth consulting on an individual basis with experienced business people volunteers — either the Service Corps of Retired Executives (SCORE) or the Active Corps of Executives (ACE). Add to this the Small Business Institute program, made up of over 20,000 business administration students. As part of their courses, they'll take on small business client problems.

Above all, any prospective small business owner should attend a one-day SBA pre-business workshop. Not only will it help you decide if you really are ready to start your business, it will help you devise a workable plan.

The SBA also has a tremendous variety of pamphlets, brochures, and other publications available. Some are for sale at a nominal cost, many are free. For publication information requests, write to: Small Business Administration, P.O. Box 15434, Fort Worth, TX 76119

For starters, request the *Women's Handbook — How SBA Can Help You Go Into Business* (# MA-5), and the two Management Assistance Publication Lists: of free publications (SBA #115-A), and those for sale (SBA #115-B).

Another handy address to note for SBA is the Office of Women Business Ownership, SBA Central Office, 1441 L Street N.W., Washington, DC 20416.

Even though you have an SBA consultation, you may find it highly advantageous to spend about $40 or $50 for an hour with someone who does ongoing work with small businesses such as the General Business Services (GBS) (with close to 1,000 business counselors across the country).

Charles Higgins, regional director for Maryland and the District of Columbia, has a number of recommendations for making such a meeting most profitable. The main one is to come prepared. Bring along any facts and figures you have developed relative to your proposed business, and a list of the questions you'd like to have answered. This way, Higgins suggests, you will be able to bounce ideas off a professional and find out which seems viable and which do not. (If you don't have a list, it's all too easy to forget the most important question until *after* you've left the office, and to reproach yourself with "why do I *always* think of what I want to say an hour later!")

Although this may be a one-time session, Higgins says that many small business people decide to become clients on an ongoing basis. (The rates for this service vary according to how extensive the counseling may be.) The reason for this is that a business counselor takes care of many things that *have* to be done, but that would probably be low-priority items on a "favorite activity" list.

Here's how Higgins describes the GBS approach: "We ask questions to determine needs, then tailor a program to meet those needs . . . set up a record-keeping system, and show them how to maintain it . . . take care of compliance with I.D. numbers and taxes, show them how to market, and provide general business counseling on an ongoing basis to help them survive and to increase their likelihood of success."

Advice from a Psychologist

Dr. S. Norman Feingold, as a psychologist and president of the National Career & Counseling Service, recognizes the importance of choosing a career that's a good match for your personality qualities *as well as your abilities.*

First of all you should have a sense of dedication and commitment. "Really believe that what you are doing will make a difference . . . and as an image consultant, it will. All too often otherwise well-qualified job applicants lose out because of physical presentation. Being in style and fashion can make a difference on the career ladder. Sometimes it may even be the major factor in the way others perceive the individual. And it's just as important for people at the top who want to stay at the top!"

Marketing Yourself

As an image consultant it is important to market *yourself* successfully. "Without this ability even high achievers face problems."

Dr. Feingold points out the importance of staying current. "Do a lot of reading so that you are aware of what's happening in your own field. Also read books or articles on sociology and psychology to keep on top of emerging lifestyle trends." (Dr. Feingold is particularily enthusiastic about membership in the World Future Society — a group devoted to improving the shape of the future.)

"Attend meetings of groups allied to your profession." (It's a good way to achieve useful information and make contacts.) Maintain good relations with others in your field. Even if there's no such thing as an image consultants' convention in your area, an informal network is helpful. No career is completely problem- or challenge-free. Knowing that others face similar challenges or problems is a tremendous help in preventing 'burn-out.' "

As a psychologist, Dr. Feingold is also aware of the other side of the career coin, the intensive enthusiasm that leads one to become a "workaholic." He recommends that however much image consultants become involved with their clients, they should be sure to "allow enough time for yourself with some kind of hobby about which you are enthused. We all need a period of change — to continue being a full multi-faceted person."

What You Can Do

1. Keep a daily notebook plan — indicating which activities should be high priority (such as the "business-getters" — making prospect calls, working on direct mail letters, doing related reading).

2. Set up a budget for related expenses on the SBA worksheet that follows.

3. Make sure you have all needed supplies.

4. Check with the Small Business Administration office nearest you to find out about free help in getting your business started.

5. Try to "network" with others in the field.

6. Use your direct mail for handouts.

7. Try advertising in neighborhood papers.

8. Offer discount coupons.

9. Check out future conventions.

10. Plan a "theme" party.

11. Work out consultant arrangements with local store or beauty shop.

12. Develop a training manual and offer classes.

The following worksheets, provided by the Small Business Administration, may be helpful when you consider starting your own business.

ESTIMATED MONTHLY EXPENSES			What to put in column 2 (These figures are typical for one kind of business, you will have to decide how many months to allow for in your business.)
Item	Your estimate of monthly expenses based on sales of $ ——— per year	Your estimate of how much cash you need to start your business (See column 3.)	
Salary of owner-manager	Column 1 $	Column 2 $	Column 3 2 times column 1
All other salaries and wages			3 times column 1
Rent			3 times column 1
Advertising			3 times column 1
Delivery expense			3 times column 1
Supplies			3 times column 1
Telephone and telegraph			3 times column 1
Other utilities			3 times column 1
Insurance			Payment required by insurance company
Taxes, including Social Security			4 times column 1
Interest			3 times column 1
Maintenance			3 times column 1
Legal and other professional fees			3 times column 1
Miscellaneous			3 times column 1

Starting Costs You Only Have to Pay Once	Column 2	
Fixtures and equipment		Suppliers will help you estimate these.
Decorating and remodeling		Talk it over with a contractor
Installation of fixtures and equipment		Talk to suppliers from whom you buy these
Starting inventory		Suppliers will help you estimate this. For total amount use typical ratio to sales.
Deposits with public utilities		Find out from utilities companies
Legal and other professional fees		Lawyer, accountant, and so on
Licenses and permits		Find out from city offices what you have to have
Advertising and promotion for opening		Estimate what you'll use
Accounts receivable		What you need to buy more stock until credit customers pay
Cash		For unexpected expenses or losses, special purchases, etc.
Other		Make a separate list and enter total
Total Estimated Cash You Need to Start With		Add up all the numbers in column 2

Chapter 4

On Your Way

A Place of Your Own

You've done your "homework" — built interest in your service — and now you're considering what kind of "office address" you need. One expense you don't have to worry about is starting out with a penthouse corner suite in the newest highrise office building in town. Think of **Mary Pennisi** who might now have 1800 square feet of studio, but who began, as she says, "on my kitchen table!"

These aren't careers that require space consuming equipment. (Although some freelance speech writers find it helpful to have a word processor and printer, there are *many* who continue to type their image-making words on paper.) Admittedly, it's not quite as easy for the public/image consultant, who may need access to videotaping and playback equipment, but a color or fashion consultant has a wide range of options. Many start out using their own homes as a favorite business base.

You may find it useful to be a semi-freelancer — someone who operates out of a store or beauty shop before going out totally on their own. You might work on a straight commission basis, or on salary plus commission — there is no set pattern. The arrangements would have to be worked out with the owner.

If you are planning to open a studio or a storefront operation, here are some factors to consider:

1. Centrally located to reach the market
2. Merchandise or raw materials available readily
3. Nearby competition situation
4. Transporation available and rates
5. Quantity of available employees
6. Prevailing rates of employee pay
7. Parking facilities
8. Adequacy of utilities (sewer, water, power, gas)
9. Traffic flow
10. Taxation burden
11. Quality of police and fire protection
12. Environmental factors (schools, cultural, community activities, enterprise of businessmen)
13. Physical suitability of building
14. Type and cost of lease
15. Provision for future expansion
16. Overall estimate of quality of site in ten years

Note: When you find a good spot, check to see whether it meets all local licensing and health code regulations. You don't want to sign a lease only to discover that you are liable to improvements in lighting or plumbing that should have been taken care of before you moved in. You might want to "snoop" around to discover why the store is vacant — have three businesses tried to make a go of it and failed in the past year? Are adjacent businesses thriving — filled with customers who could also stop in your shop? Better locations may sport higher rents, but they may be worth it to you.

Public Exposure

Whatever kind of office arrangement you decide upon, it is vital that you continue to market yourself and keep your consulting service in the public eye. There are a number of ways to do this.

Those who stage charitable events are on the lookout for auction, raffle, or door prizes. Offering your services as a door prize won't result in an immediate jackpot, but it can give your name additional recognition, and is a strategy you should consider in connection with charity events that receive good media coverage.

Every single time you get public exposure you're going to be judged, so make sure you *always* look and act the way a top-notch image-maker should, but don't get carried away with yourself as being the *only* arbiter available! Constantly keep your goals in mind, and see what you can do each day to bring yourself a little closer to reaching them as you plan the next set.

Welcome opportunities to speak before groups (even if a number of these occasions are for good will rather than dollars). Also consider such "good deeds" as demonstrations in retirement homes. Many are looking for activities to interest their residents, and these older people like to look their best too.

See if you can't persuade a talk-show hostess to let you color-drape her on TV. It makes fascinating viewing to show how different colors relate to television lighting, and would be a valuable taping for use by clubs and organizations whose members frequently appear on television.

Building a Name

How do you go about building your name so that you attract clients? Public image consultant **James Gray** has these recommendations:

1. "Make sure that you really have the knowledge about your subject, and enough experience to make your consultation of value.

2. Have a willingness to work with people. Take the time to listen to where your clients are going so that you will know what their real needs are.

3. Be persistent. You'll need this persistence on several levels. Of course, it is essential when you are trying to market yourself, but there is much more."

It is important that you get good training. Most areas have continuing education courses, but if what you need isn't taught in your locale, it's worthwhile to check out its availability in the nearest city to make sure you study with someone who is respected.

Once you have the training, Gray recommends, continue to keep up on trends by reading and by continuing to promote yourself. One way is to join respected organizations in your area such as the local chamber of commerce, the political party of your choice, or other community groups allied to your interests. Go to places where you can make contact with people who share common concerns.

And, above all, Gray says, "always respect the client. Never take anyone lightly or get to the point where you feel you can breeze over a request. Build a solid core. It's better to turn down a client or speaking engagement than to accept and create a bad impression. The best road to success is a reputation for doing a great job — *every time!*"

Customer Orientation

Public image consultant **Lou Hampton** stresses the importance of "customer orientation." What a consultant offers isn't a product —

it is a service. "Go out and talk with people. Focus on how your consultation can apply, and put the emphasis on that appeal. I also believe that any person who is a speech/image consultant should get out and make speeches! I'm a little uncomfortable with those who don't."

"Consultants — for color or fashion as well as public-image speaking — or anyone who has to do a fair amount of speaking, would find the National Speakers Association useful. They have three different tracks of programming for their conventions and workshops — for the newcomer, the more established, and the advanced speaker. Attendees find the organization an amazingly open group for such a competitive business. Members are very interested in helping one another, knowing which things work and which don't, and exchanging ideas. Not only are these meetings a good source of contacts, but, if you're good, sometimes a source of referrals as well."

Persistence

Author **Ruthanne Olds** speaks of persistence, and how it applied to her. "It took me a while to get started, but I kept at it, continued giving talks on the importance of image, got local organizations' mailing lists so that I could do direct mail to my target market — career-minded women, age 20 to approximately 55 or 60."

"To make a go of image consulting it is necessary to be as visible as possible so I wrote a bylined fashion column, combined modeling (she had been a large-size model) with image consulting . . . and the client list began to grow."

Carole Jackson believes in giving 110 percent to any project associated with her. Before she began working on her book, she took leave from teaching to study the best ways to present color ideas through the printing process . . . even working with a printer on an intensive study of color separation and printing.

Contacting Local Businesses

Color consultant **Doris Pooser** notes that more and more organizations are beginning to recognize the importance of the right image at every level. "Money spent on improving one's image is considered a good investment, rather than a frivolous money-waster. Companies such as Community Federal Bank of Virginia and State Farm Insurance, for example, recently arranged self-image seminars for their entire female staff. I look forward to giving more classes for men. They too have a need to improve their image and credibility."

As an in-store fashion consultant, **Gerry Kendall** finds her career clients falling into three categories: 1) Recent graduates who are smart enough to know the campus "uniform" of T-shirt and jeans is a no-no in the professional world, 2) Upwardly mobile women who have worked for several years and recognize the need for their fashion image to keep pace with their career development, and 3) Key executives who are too busy for fashion browsing, and feel they don't even have time to think about wardrobe plans. Even though their fashion budget has expanded considerably, the "bottom line" still counts.

"Most of these people continue as clients with their fashion consultant, progressing from one category to the next. The longer the teamwork, the better the consultant knows the client and which wardrobe categories should be given priorities. Consultants are used for convenience and know-how . . . to help achieve the best for the fashion dollar."

Coping with Pressure

Image consultant **Brenda York** stresses that everyone in this field has to be prepared to take pressure. "There's the variety of reactions you may face from people when you mention your profession. Some may be hostile: 'Image . . . what a plastic profession!' Others are apologetic every time they see you afterwards, 'Oh, I'd hoped I wouldn't run into you looking like **this!**' There's also the need to concentrate on constantly looking like an image consultant . . . even if you just run into the grocery store to pick up a couple of items!"

She also mentions that you should maintain your confidence, and have a manner that's diplomatic — but firm.

Mary Pennisi points out that anyone interested in the upward success route in a consultancy should recognize that: "integrity, perseverence and dedication can go a long way, but there's not such thing as 'overnight success.' One has to plan on long hours and hard work, and be prepared for some big disappointments along the way. However, there usually are ways you can use 'Yankee Ingenuity' to find the rainbow . . . because there's also a very great deal of satisfaction you'll derive from being a color/image consultant."

Problem-Solving

Deanna Radeloff is one of those people who has risen above a situation that could have caused her to give up her entire enterprise.

Even when everything points to success, problems can arise. Radeloff developed an entirely new color system, in which she invested approximately $70,000 in materials, and it seemed worth it because of the reaction she was receiving. She began training others. (A local ad drew 41 responses of interest in her 40-hour certification training course.) The idea intrigued network television, and she was asked to appear to explain her idea.

Then the nightmare hit! She received a letter from an Atlanta company saying that she was using a name *they* had registered, and must stop *immediately*. "Needless to say, I was more than disturbed, particularly when I had hired an ad agency to come up with the name — and a law firm to research it! There I was with 14,000 color wheels, 225 sets of training materials, radio cassettes, labels, etc., etc. — all with a name I could no longer use! My husband and I went to Atlanta, but recognized that my concept was quite different from theirs. We had to face two new questions: Do we assume the major loss in materials, revamp them, and go on? . . . or is it worth the effort?"

"My consultants encouraged me, 'Dee, you *have* to continue! What you have is so good — it works so well!' After many a sleepless night, I decided I couldn't give up what I had developed. With much deliberation, the new ColorConcept 7™ name was chosen, and we're now changing the materials. Through it all, however, it's been satisfying to see the way interest has been growing in what we offer. While I have had to slow down a bit when school's in session, I have trained a number of consultants, and seen the way these people appreciate what makes the program unique: the fact that it is a *teaching* program. When they finish their intensified study using a color wheel, they must teach color to 3-5 clients before they are certified."

To Be or Not to Be . . . An Advertiser

Sooner or later the question of advertising arises. Most consultants, such as **Carole Jackson** and **Leatrice Eiseman,** find that word of mouth is what really sells. There's no doubt that the satisfied client who tells others *is* your best testimonial, but you can't always wait for that even though **Brenda York** says, "Don't bother with a lot of advertising. You'll get better results through press releases and publicity."

A move to Wichita, Kansas brought special challenges to New Jersey-born **Verdale Benjamin.** "People, customs, habits, and lifestyles are different from my own. I'm a newcomer bringing a new concept, a new service to a community that is steeped in time-honored tradition. It is important that I market my service creatively." When she started out, Benjamin says that her greatest expense was advertising and effective business promotions. "It continues to be today."

Some advertising ideas that may be useful for you are:

- Have a direct mail brochure prepared, and use it for more than mailings. It makes a good handout at your seminars, or for potential clients who may stop by your office.

- Special mailings. **Ruthanne Olds** suggests that you get lists of the kinds of organizations or clubs with members who seem like good prospects. Even if you don't belong, you're likely to have some friends who do.

Since mailings cost money, it is especially important that you target your audience to get a high rate of return (keep in mind that a 2 percent rate — or just one response to 50 things sent — is considered a *very good* response and you'll see how much could be wasted if you made a *very wrong* guess). Unfortunately it is impossible to be 100 percent sure in advance about what will work and what won't.

If you do discover an approach that really "clicks," however, don't hesitate to repeat it with another group. When you do mailings, you have to decide whether to send a letter alone, or include your brochure if you have one. When you're having printing done, be sure to tell your printer what your plans are. See if the printer can't make suggestions that might save you money on stock weight and envelopes without costing you a good impression.

A less formal advertising method is to post your card, brochure, or even a poster on apartment building bulletin boards or in college activity centers. In conjunction with this, makeup consultants might not only ask photographers to post their cards, but work out special arrangements to do "important occasion photographic makeups" for their subjects.

Until you begin to show a profit, you may want to write your own ads. Keep the following advice in mind.

- Make sure the reader is given all necessary information (Who-What-Where-When-Why-How) — in the clearest, most logical and orderly arrangement possible.

- Guard against factual errors; if you find mistakes and you know they are mistakes, correct them.

- Correct all errors in grammar, punctuation, and spelling. Pay special attention to names, addresses, and figures. Check definitions and quotations.

- Watch out for double or ambiguous meanings and unconscious humor.

- Put yourself in the intended reader's place — watch the *tone* as well as the meaning. Guard against bad taste, officiousness, or other offensiveness. Read for the *connotation* (emotional overtone) as well as the *denotation* (definition) of words.

- Edit first for clarity and precision of meaning, then for conciseness of expression.

- Pay close attention to *format*. Help the reader get a *handle* by using appropriate typographical devices: headings, subheadings, bullets, numbered or lettered listings, italicized words, and indented paragraphs.

- Add all figures to ensure that arithmetic is correct and consistent.

Sometimes an image consultant may become a client herself for a specialized type of promotional advertising. As an example, there's **Lisa Rich.** The students who get public/image training as well as voice instruction from her may think of Rich as a "coach." However, she is also an up-and-coming jazz singer who recently cut her first album, "Listen Here," for the Tritone Records label.

To make sure the album attracted record-store browsers by conveying the image *she* wanted, Rich went beyond talking with other musicians about the reactions their albums had received. She consulted a model-agency owner who specializes in visual typing. (In other words, don't overlook *anyone* as a potential client!)

When you decide you need what most people consider "real" advertising — the print media — try a small-scale test with one of your "neighborhood" papers for several reasons. First, it's a good way to concentrate on people in your area . . . it isn't as likely to get "lost" as a small ad would in a metropolitan multi-section Sunday edition, and it certainly wouldn't be as expensive. (Speaking of expensive, cost was the reason that none of the consultants we interviewed mentioned television or radio advertising. They try, and you can as well, to get *on* the shows.)

Sometimes a gamble on a larger investment *does* pay off. **Mary Pennisi** spent $250 to spread the word about the store seminars she would be presenting. She got enough clients to keep her busy for more than ten months, but something like this doesn't happen that often.

An idea which might be considered more "promotion" than "advertising" is to have gift certificates or discount coupons printed. Particularly in towns or smaller cities, you'll find that you get good response when they're left at beauty salons, libraries, neighborhood grocery stores' bulletin boards . . . or sent to women's clubs. As an incentive for clients who refer a certain number of friends for consultation, consider some kind of special little gift.

Client Multipliers (the kind that do your budget — and your heart — good)

Inevitably there's bound to be a lull time. Frustrating as this may seem at the time, it offers an opportunity to "meditate." Do your own brainstorming *without* censoring any thought! Write down every possibility about people or organizations that might be potential clients . . . what you *could* do to attract these people that you haven't done.

As you sift through the ideas, a number may strike you as too impractical, expensive, or just plain ridiculous. On the other hand, you'll be surprised at the quantity of *effective* remainders. Don't stop at writing them down, do them!

Here are some idea-starters: What about future conventions in your area? Your local chamber of commerce or board of trade is likely to have a list (in Washington, D.C., such a list covers a three-year period, and includes projected attendance, which gives an idea of those most likely to be interested in having programs to attract a variety of interests). Also contact the convention center, armory, or hotels that seem to have a large number of conventions, to check on future bookings. Then write to the different organizations' convention-coordinators or planners, and suggest that you offer a presentation or seminar on your specialty. Getting the first one may be the hardest, but after that you'll find that the statement "success builds on success" is more truth than cliche. Such presentations are increasingly becoming part of convention packages because putting on a good popular presentation is in everyone's interest.

Shifting from groups to the individual, what about suggesting a gift certificate for your service as a graduation present? Many consultants find that gift certificates around special holidays are good business-boosters. They also show a great deal more "you're special" attention than the usual Mother's Day or Father's Day present! (We know of one woman who was so thrilled with the reactions she received after she had her own colors done that she couldn't think of a better engagement present for a young friend than to give her a color consultation! Many others may feel the same way so keep alert to engagement announcements in the papers. And keep in mind that if *both* members of the couple know what *their* colors are, it may well prevent a lot of color decorating "discussions" later.)

Target certain professions for special mailings . . . particularly those whose livelihood frequently depends upon public reaction. And follow up your mailings with telephone calls whenever possible.

Make sure that the organizations with the largest number of employees know about you. While smaller organizations may provide some business, the bigger ones are likely to have some kind of organized employee relations program. Convince them to let you put on a seminar. (Naturally your fee for any large group will be considerably higher than for a small group of individuals.)

Do Your Homework

Before you present your proposal, have an idea of what this rate should be to make it profitable to you and fair to the organization. You don't want to place yourself in the position of being asked this question and having to mutter, "Uh, I've never done one of these . . . let me think about it." Say something like that and you're likely to *continue* having done none! Once again, that familiar word — homework — can prevent such a situation. Find out what the going rate is for such presentations by talking to others in the field, learn what specific organizations usually allot to individual events of the employee program by estimating costs of past events of a similar nature, and have this information firmly in mind when you go in to give your proposal.

Color consultants might attract publicity by staging a "Come as Your Season" costume party. Speaking of publicity, image consultant **Brenda York** recommends being photographed whenever you do "public activities" such as teaching, demonstrations, or whatever. There are two reasons for this. One, of course, is that such pictures will certainly make your portfolio more impressive. The other is that they will provide handy proof of the need for certain business expenditures (such as color drapes) at tax time.

Get to know the key people in local stores — work out arrangements for doing special displays or promotions, or training employees. You might go even further, as **Holly Sallade** does, and advise organizations on colors for uniforms, logos, and interiors.

Chapter 5

When You Aren't Quite Ready To Tackle The World Alone

Join an Organization that Works for You

For a number of people the idea of becoming an independent image consultant may still seem a little intimidating . . . particularly if you haven't dealt with a variety of working environments and situations.

One solution to the transition problem is to work with a direct selling organization. Several million women in this country already are. That's why one of them recommended it for "taking that first step into the real world."

There are *many* direct selling organizations — some 130 belong to the Direct Selling Association. However, since this book is about image, we have spoken to representatives of two beauty products organizations. (While a number of others may have fine beauty products, overall they are known for their diversified items.)

When Part-time Is Enough

Rebecca Mead has a full-time museum education job that she loves, but for the past few months she's also been a part-time Avon representative. A personal priority had made it necessary for her to be at home in the early afternoon. Her employer agreed to let her work fewer hours, but that cut her salary. "I wanted to make up this money, and needed something that would provide extra income yet let me dictate my working time availability. I liked the Avon products and knew they had a good guarantee so I decided to become an Avon representative.

Starting out does take some courage because every 'no' seems a personal rejection. But if you keep trying, then it's worth it. As a person interested in paleontology, it reminded me of fossil hunting. When you go out collecting, you can't find a single fossil in the beginning — then after you've seen one, you find a lot! It just takes perserverance and a willingness to keep doing it without losing your self-confidence."

Ms. Mead says that her husband wondered at first why she spent at least an hour with each customer. "But it's like any business. I think you want to put your heart and soul in it. Once you're organized and have things perking along you're able to shorten somewhat, but still want to give it quality time. Although I've been offered the opportunity to be an Avon area leader, I don't feel that I should make that commitment just yet. Part-time is fine . . . for the supplemental money *and* for the fun of it!"

A Career that Builds Friendships

Someone who's been with Avon for years instead of months is **Pat McCormack.** She's currently a district manager, but started selling the products when her husband was in graduate school getting his doctorate.

"Since we'd had years of getting along on a student's budget I didn't really do it for the money. In fact, my husband's first question was, 'Aren't I making enough?' I told him that I thought this was something a 'fulltime mother' could work into her schedule.

At that time our daughter was the only one of our children who hadn't started school, so I worked out a one-day-a-week babysitting tradeoff arrangement with one of the neighbors on the block . . . and it was great for the children as well as for us.

I'd known the Avon products and liked them, now I discovered how good Avon was about providing training information and free makeup seminars. As I did more and more direct selling, my self-confidence grew.

Sometimes being a wife and mother means being so absorbed in others' lives that one doesn't fully appreciate her own worth. Getting out and talking with new people helps this. I'd definitely recommend it! For anyone who is interested in this field, your representative will be glad to talk with you. (And if you don't have a representative, check the local phone book for the organization's listing or the ads in magazines.)

Selling at work may be easier than the challenges of metropolitan home areas where it's necessary to synchronize schedules, but anyone who thinks a rural area might be a less promising market is wrong.

People there are excellent prospects . . . really appreciate the representative's visits and the personal service provided, so much so that real friendships frequently develop.

It's nice to be able to take pride in the company for which you work. When I think of what it's done for me — a quiet wife and mother — I know that other women as well would find it an excellent lifestyle."

Satisfied Customer to Sales Director

Shula Davis of Sterling, Virginia had been a high school mathematics teacher for thirty-five years when she happened to see a cosmetics demonstration in a Reston mall. A Mary Kay consultant was giving facials, and Ms. Davis went over to watch.

"The woman just bloomed, and I asked her, 'Can you do me too?' Since it was the end of the day, it wasn't possible then, but she offered to set up an appointment at my home.

After having my facial, I liked the products so much that I continued to order from her. Then she moved away and I was running out of supplies about the time we were planning to move to a new area. No one around there seemed to have heard of Mary Kay, and I was beginning to feel rather desperate, since I didn't want to give up their products. I finally called corporate headquarters in Dallas. When they found out it was a regular call, they gave me the toll-free number and had me call back. When I did, they not only told me where the nearest consultant was located, but asked if I'd be interested in becoming a salesperson. My reaction was, 'Maybe I would!'

I received my information and the nearby representative also got in touch with me. I immediately became interested . . . especially after accepting her invitation to attend a Mary Kay function. From that point, I participated in their full-time free training program which included learning how to give facials and analyze skin types, choose facial designs and make sure the makeup is matched suitably to the face. In addition to what might be considered artistic training, there also was the practical training an independent business person needs: how to book and hold shows, to recruit and manage other consultants. I observed three sessions, attended the basic training class, worked with a seasoned consultant, and did the other things that are part of Mary Kay training . . . booked eight shows while waiting for my kit to arrive, and held five shows in the first two weeks after I received it."

Ms. Davis, a Mary Kay consultant since 1977, has never regretted her decision. She has been promoted from Consultant to Sales Director.

For anyone interested in doing as she has, Shula Davis recommends that the person contact her local Mary Kay consultant. (You can find her telephone number under "Mary Kay" in the phone book.) The former math teacher feels that it's something that definitely adds up the right way. "I count this as my second *career!*"

Losing One Job Opens New Opportunity

Being fired as a secretary turned out to be the best thing that ever happened to **Thomacine Pleasure!** Always interested in the arts, she decided to study voice at her local university. She was so impressed by her voice teacher's complexion that she asked her what her secret was! It turned out that she credited the Mary Kay products which she also sold part time.

"I became interested in doing this myself and started selling part-time. Once involved it was great! Within two or three months my business volume was growing rapidly. Then I went to the annual seminar, and that inspired me even more . . . learning what others around the country were doing, how to set even higher goals."

Now after several years, Thomacine Pleasure is recognized in the nation's capital by the pink Cadillac she drives . . . symbol of those whose sales volume is recognized by the Mary Kay organization as being "Cadillac-level."Thomacine Pleasure has also trained others to be successful themselves.

While at some time she may go back to the arts, which were her first love, Ms. Pleasure says: "This business has exposed me to *many* things from music to design in general; but I know that when you're selling products you really believe in, it can be the best shot for women I've ever seen!"

Guidelines for Potential Direct Sales Persons

Before becoming a direct sales person for any organization, the national Direct Selling Association suggests that you consider a few guidelines:

- Choose a product you like and will find easy to explain and demonstrate.

- Be sure to get all of the facts on commissions, responsibilities, expenses and time requirements.

- Avoid plans promising easy income quickly. Your earnings are directly related to the time and effort you put into your work.

- If an investment is required, make sure it's for a starter or sample kit, and look into what rights you have to return the kit should you change your mind about direct selling.

- Check into other costs.

- Most direct selling firms offer excellent training sessions and you'll do well to attend them. You'll learn the basics from company literature and get on-the-job training from the person who recruited you.

- Check into company guarantees and return policies . . . they're important to your customer.

- Have a good attitude. Enthusiasm for the product you're selling, the company you represent and the people you meet will help you succeed in direct selling.

Most reputable direct selling companies are members of the Direct Selling Association. If you'd like a current membership listing which includes addresses, telephone numbers and product lines, send a legal-size stamped, self-addressed envelope to the Direct Selling Association, Dept. IK, 1730 M Street, N. W., Washington, D. C. 20036.

What You Can Do

1. Write to the Direct Selling Association for its member list.

2. Follow-up by contacting companies of greatest interest to you.

3. Arrange to meet with their local representatives (if you don't have your own representative) and find out what it's actually like to do this . . . how they started, any problems they had in the beginning, what kind of schedule you should plan on, etc. (In other words, ask for an "informational interview.")

Chapter 6

The Success Pyramid

Pyramiding Your Success

You've made your mark as an image consultant to the point where you are receiving almost as many "how do you do it?" questions as client calls.

There are a number of ways for you to pyramid your success. First, and foremost, be sure to keep your name before the public. This way potential clients are more likely to hear about you, and past clients will have no hesitancy about continuing to recommend you because it's obvious that you are definitely "staying current."

Many successful consultants continue to do such things as teaching adult education classes. It isn't for the money, which is far less than their regular fees. They find it an excellent way to get that public exposure.

Finding Help

As you continue to add to your client list, you may find that you need someone to assist you with your schedule, or to open a branch location in a nearby town, or to expand into other areas. How do you find someone who can provide the right credentials?

If you haven't been keeping a list of people who have called and expressed an interest in becoming a consultant, start now. Also consider developing a curriculum for your own training course.

Make sure that it is well thought out before you offer it, and that you can arrange to block out time to make it available. When everything is organized and available to interested parties, you will find that your training course serves several purposes.

It provides a wanted service. It keeps your name before the public, and brings in some additional income. It also offers a far better way to screen prospective assistants than just running a classified "help wanted" ad.

Branching Out

When you're considering opening a branch location, check out several areas *before* you make a decision, by market-testing client potential and making sure that the community isn't currently consultant-saturated. If it continues to look good after you have done your preliminary detective work, go full tilt into the selection of appropriate space, and appropriate publicizing of your new, additional location. However, it really is a case of look once, then look twice again before you leap!

Becoming a Media Personality

Consider becoming a media personality. Try writing up a sample column or two, to see how easily it flows. In addition to explaining a little about general principles of your craft, you might include an interesting anecdote or two from your files (protecting the client's privacy by changing name and identifying circumstances), and a question-and-answer section. Do an audio version for radio, as well.

If you've already appeared on TV, see if you can't get a copy of the videotape. If you haven't, it would be worth your time to have an "audition sample" made. Then, when you go to the newspaper office or the radio or TV studio for an interview, you will come prepared.

Another useful method of preparation is the development of a presentation that incorporates facts or figures indicating the growth of interest in your service — and the potential interest of their market (whether readers, listeners, or viewers). If you can "sell" them on the "ratings," you're much more likely to get a favorable response than if you just appear with a "here I am" attitude.

Media interest in the field of image consultancy is growing rapidly. One person we interviewed had been asked to discuss a specific subject on a TV talk show. When they were off the air, the hostess asked: "You *will* fly back for another appearance? . . . Our viewers are so interested in what you do!"

Clare Miller says that at each level of success growth there is some high point that makes you realize you've "made it." One for her has to be "the first time I addressed an international audience and experienced that funny pause while translators in special booths bridged the language barriers for me. The audience response is particularly interesting, returning unevenly, as the translations play out."

Workshops, Lectures, Travel

Lynda Rosenberg uses her own training and experience to think of ways to accommodate her clients and expand her business. Among the ideas that she's turned into reality are follow-up workshops on wardrobe, makeup, and skin care, and developing the fast-growing men's market with an in-depth slide presentation and collection of swatches suitable for sports coats and suitings. She also works with several area boutiques to train their sales staffs on ways to color-coordinate available fashions with the customer's own color swatches.

Following her own advice, **Holly Sallade** is building an areawide network of color consultants ("I've turned down some whom I didn't feel had the right background to help clients") and is reaching her goal of expanding Color My Image, Ltd. into other states. "So far I have Texas, Maryland, and the Chicago area of Illinois, as well as my own area."

Today **Ruthanne Olds** is the owner of Image Communications Co., and author of *Big & Beautiful*. She's also a nationally known fashion coordinator/lecturer who spends a great deal of time giving seminars around the country.

"My book is the outgrowth of the image communications work I've been doing with groups and individuals, and I am pleased that people consider me successful for what I've accomplished. However, my personal standards say 'give me five more years!' My next goal is to build a staff of qualified consultants in this special field, an entire organization devoted to helping the larger-size woman achieve the positive image she should concentrate on presenting."

Popular speaker **Doris Pooser** has traveled to conventions from West Palm Beach to The Greenbrier in West Virginia, and says, "As much as I enjoy the one-to-one of class seminars where the results can be seen instantly, I'm so pleased to be training as well. It's a wonderful opportunity to reach so many more people."

It's obvious that **Cindy Harsley** overcame her old problem of organizing time when she started out as a fashion consultant. Today her work schedule is a tale of two cities — commuting between Washington and New York. In addition to working with her individual clients, she also handles a variety of special image projects that relate to fashion marketing, advises on packaging and ways to get publicity, works with a hair salon to establish the important beginning-of-the-season image focus, and has styled a magazine cover for *The Washingtonian* and a men's fashion layout for *Regardie's*.

With all of these activities, it's easy to see that Harsley has a special joy in her work as a "persnickety" fashion consultant. "According to **Diana Vreeland**, 'true style is something a person either has or doesn't have.' It's also true that *each* person has his or her own personal style. A fashion-image consultant can help develop it by suggesting ways to wear something, combine colors or accessorize so that her client not only will look great, but say, 'Oh, I never would have thought of that!' "

Leatrice Eiseman says that one of her greatest career satisfactions has been the publication of *Alive with Color*. "Although intended for individual use, I feel that it is a useful information source for those who want to be consultants."

For freelance fashion consultant **Helen Moody**, the success pyramid meant expanding into TV fashion consultation. "A lot of my friends now work in TV and are interested in looking their best always. In TV dressing, the very first thing for a woman or man to consider is the hair. If it isn't the right color and length it can distract from everything else. Next comes the neckline, which should be chosen to frame the face. After that I consider the color of the fashion. Although I keep my clients' names confidential, I work with newspeople, talk show hosts, and specialty show performers."

Moody has also gotten into attorney-consultations. "I advise them on what their clients should wear in court. I'm firmly convinced that **Jean Harris** wouldn't be in jail today if she'd worn something different that first day — a simple dark dress with a white collar, and carried a handkerchief that she would continue to wring in her hands. That mink hat was too much 'bad lady of the manor' and too little 'wronged headmistress' for the jury!"

"A consultant should know how to be her own best and most constant critic . . . always sharpening her perception of what works in fashion. Once the kind of fashion statement decision is made, do it! You can't let yourself be invisible if relying on word of mouth referrals! People have to know who you are, what kind of fashion image is your specialty."

It is interesting to see how much can happen in a decade to someone as innovative a teacher-communicator as **Carole Jackson.** *Color Me Beautiful* is setting new records for consecutive appearances on the best-seller list. Jackson is chairman of the board of a multi-million dollar corporation, and has an international network of carefully selected, authorized "Color Me Beautiful" consultants in this country and abroad.

Fashion consultant **Nancy Thompson** says that she originally "planned to go into women's homes, but was convinced by women needing professional wardrobe consultation that my major market was the corporate world."

Since few CEOs of major corporations are interested in a fashion-show approach, Thompson had to convince them of the bottom-line value of her seminars. Employees who exude an air of confidence and well-placed power are a definite credit to their organization.

Thompson's success is reflected in the special niche she has achieved. Her client list includes corporations, government agencies, private individuals and organizations, and public figures such as political candidates and their spouses.

Studying the Trends

It's impossible to overemphasize the importance of being *really aware.* Know what's going on in the field, get a feeling for emerging trends by reading and finding out what other consultants are doing that works successfully. Be ready to take advantage of the unexpected business or educational opportunity, or training referral.

It's worthwhile to join an association that relates to your field, or a broad umbrella group such as the newly formed International Institute of Professional Image Consultants.

In any case, you couldn't choose a better time than NOW to become an image consultant. It *really is* the hot new career option of the years just ahead!

Now, sit down and "talk" to the experts on the following pages. They've all had different backgrounds and assorted starting points and developed exciting careers as consultants in color, fashion, or public image. Here they talk frankly about how they did it . . .

What You Can Do

1. Keep an up-to-date client list for future mailings.

2. Teach adult education classes.

3. Write a newspaper column.

4. Prepare an audition tape for radio or TV.

5. Think of ways to expand your operation.

6. Check out possible branch locations (but carefully market-test before you sign any lease).

7. Offer follow-up workshops.

PART II

Talking To The Experts

Chapter 7

The Color Consultants

LEATRICE EISEMAN:
Alive with Color!
Color Can Change Your Life

Color authority and author **Leatrice Eiseman** is a strong believer in the psychology of color — has seen its effect on moods, memories, and even marriages!

Prior to her own marriage, she was director of education for a group of east coast self-improvement schools. As part of her job she trained teachers, did fashion shows, wrote the curriculum, and appeared on radio and TV.

Moving to California with her husband, she began working with a leading west coast specialty store and also went back to school for advanced training in psychology — a certificate in counseling from U.C.L.A.

A Part-time Solution

After the birth of her first child, she wanted to work part-time. Looking for a way to continue using her background and talent, she thought of the San Fernando Valley's occupational training center. It had been established to help engineers (and their families) who were suffering the down side of a boom-or-bust occupation. Divorces were commonplace due to emotional and financial stresses, and many former wives suddenly found themselves facing serious financial problems for the first time. The center was teaching them skills, but they needed the confidence to establish or revive a successful self-image.

Eiseman convinced the school's director that a course in "Face, Figure, and Fashion" would help. There wasn't much time to work out her curriculum plans but she did it, and was ready when September arrived. "It turned out to be such a great, satisfying experience that I remained there for ten years, working part-time while my son and daughter were growing up. Then I decided to spread my wings. My husband encouraged me, with the stipulation that I get live-in help. That was my greatest financial expense, but was a tremendous help. In time, my greatest expense was in making contacts — the phone calls, the many letters. However, one needs to think of this as part of the investment. It's really an absolute necessity for the build-up."

An Intensely Creative Experience

"My first Sunrise, Sunlight, and Sunset palettes were a labor of love, but looked far different from the uniform way they appear in my new book, *Alive with Color*. I took my color samples from every source — swatches, clipped photographs, and ads. Even now I encourage clients to make their collages. Bring in a picture of how you see yourself as a person, your fantasies, ultimate goals, who you are — and who you want to be! It's an intensely creative experience that encourages individual flair."

"When I was 'getting it together,' I would have loved a course in consulting. Instead, I had to do it by feeling my way. Today there are courses . . . I provide training myself. I also believe that it's good to build up additional confidence by considering something such as psychology, public speaking, self-improvement, interior design, or any course that has something to do with the arts. Both as a teacher and as a student, I'm a great believer in adult education."

A Continuing Need for Color/Image Consultants

"As with any career field, some who choose to enter this area may become discouraged and think that they'd be happier doing something else. However, it is a field that encourages talent — is very satisfying to see 'the cream rising.' "

CAROLE JACKSON:
The Hue Guru
A "Winter" Wonder

Ten years ago the idea of being considered a color "guru" was the farthest thought from **Carole Jackson's** mind. "I was a full-time housewife with two small children. If I had any career aspirations at that time, they were to go into psychology or perhaps social work."

Painting had always been a hobby of this Stanford University honors graduate, but was she concerned about the effects of color at that time? "Only in terms of my art work." That all changed for her when she went to California to visit family and friends. Her sister encouraged her to have her colors done, and she was told that she was a "Winter," and given some paper swatches of vivid icy colors. When she returned to Washington, she started experimenting with wearing "her" colors.

Playing Color Analyst to your Friends

The results were so complimentary that she began playing color analyst to her friends. "At the same time I'd also begun to study interior decorating and to sell my art to New York's Madison Avenue galleries. Each new achievement convinced me that I did have a talent for using color, and prompted my decision to leave home for several months and study at the Fashion Academy in Costa Mesa, California."

From "Carole Cookie" to "Carole Color"

Then her husband was transferred to New York, and they moved to Mt. Kisco. Since Jackson at that time knew absolutely no one there, she decided to pass the time by volunteering to teach a cookie-art workshop at the local Junior League. In this unlikely setting a whole new career was born when she happened to casually mention during class, "Oh, by the way, I just learned how to tell people what colors look good on them." INSTANTLY her first class was filled, and she was destined to be known not as "Carole Cookie" (which might have happened!) but as "Carole Color" far beyond the boundaries of Mt. Kisco.

The Magic of "Color Me Beautiful"

The first classes were held in her own home, but her success soon called for larger space. She rented a studio, called her business "The Fashion Studio," which later became "Personal Design," a name she continued to use when she moved to Virginia. After the successful publication of her book in 1980, she adopted its "Color Me Beautiful" name, which she incorporated and trademarked. The book had come about because of her desire to enable more people to enjoy the "magic" of seeing what happens whenever they wear "their" colors.

JoAnne Nicolson:
Personalizing Color

300 Strong

Although **JoAnne Nicholson** lives in Washington, D.C., and her partner, **Judy Lewis-Crum,** in California, their COLOR 1 Associates Inc. goes *far* beyond these areas. They now have over 300 associates — in all 50 states as well as in Canada, Australia, France, the Philippines, Singapore, Japan, and Israel.

"Judy and I started charting in 1968. When we first had the idea of creating a personalized color service, there was very little that was helpful to read. By the time we had incorporated in 1977, we had spent more than nine years developing a system of personal color-use based on the individual's natural body coloring."

The two partners met as models in southern California. Lewis-Crum, who later became COLOR 1's chairman of the board, had graduated with honors from the University of California. Her degree was in art and education, and she later taught as well as modeled. Nicholson, president of the far-flung operation, studied at the University of Nevada, and had a background in fashion journalism, fashion coordination, modeling, and color and wardrobe teaching.

You Don't Need a Fashion Background

Interestingly enough, although both Nicholson and Lewis-Crum come from fashion and beauty backgrounds, they don't strive to find people with similar experience. "Many have preconceived notions about color that they have to work through. Most of our associates have been teachers and are people who have a love of color they want to express in a full-time career. They range in age from 20 to the early 70's, and come from many different backgrounds."

Nicholson's advice to anyone starting out in the color/image consultant field is: "Make sure you get comprehensive training before you start advising people — and make sure you totally believe in the concept you will be asking your clients to use."

In line with the philosophy of others who have observed the difference the right colors make in a person's appearance and attitudes, she is enthusiastic about what happens: "It's such a satisfaction — the knowledge that it absolutely changes one's life! Some women worry about spending the money on themselves for a consultation. What they're actually doing is investing . . . they learn how to make every dollar count in the clothes and makeup they select, and will never again waste money on 'losers.' "

DORIS POOSER:
Traveling on Color
Taking Color to Tokyo

Lynchburg, Virginia housewife **Doris Pooser** first heard about "Color Me Beautiful" when she and her family were living in London. "I had been taking some color-analysis classes, then heard of Carole Jackson's book. Since our next destination was Japan, where we were to spend two years, I was interested in taking her concept to Tokyo."

I wrote her for permission and she suggested that I get in touch with her publisher. When we returned to the states, the three of us met and she agreed to train me to represent 'Color Me Beautiful' in Japan.

Not Just Interested in Money

Jackson is very conscious of her clients' needs and sympathetic to them; she always wants to make sure that her consultants also place the clients' interests first, and are not merely interested in making money. That's why she interviews potential consultants carefully. The selection process is rigorous. They then go through an intensive 10-day training course after they pass the color test.

After I took the training program I edited and rewrote the book for Japanese use — blue-eyed blondes aren't that common a sight among Japanese color and fashion types! It was a very exciting experience working with these women. They are so wonderfully fashion-conscious that we frequently forget that the nation has been Western-ized for such a short time.

Although they have great fashion designers, many needed help with wardrobe planning. Color is *very* important. They are quick to notice one another's 'season,' and to sense the difference in clothing person-ality types from 'sporty-natural' to 'dramatic,' etc.

What characteristics do I think a consultant should have? First of all, what everyone defines as that eye for color. Without this, nothing much is possible. Next, a definite caring and understanding of people, a neat, up-to-date appearance, and charisma.

Some dermatologists have machines that can measure the exact degree of yellow or blue in the skin, but machines can't be caring, or deal with individuals who have unusual combinations of coloring.

Obviously one has to start *somewhere* to plan a good wardrobe — why not with color? As a math major who later taught, I particularly appreciate this orderly approach to something that we don't always deal with in an orderly manner."

Using Math in Fashion

Pooser's early interest in fashion was stimulated by the career of her mother, who held a variety of responsible positions in New York's fashion industry. Although Pooser chose math for her own career, she continued to be an avid reader of such publications as *W* and *Vogue*, and to study fashion and interior design.

"In teaching algebra and geometry I'd loved the feeling of communicating the points to students . . . in fashion I had always enjoyed sewing and modeling, and certainly found it exciting working with American and Japanese designers in Japan. Then, suddenly, when I began working with 'Color Me Beautiful,' *all* the pieces fit! Now I am teaching a logical approach to helping people look good and feel good about themselves."

HOLLY SALLADE:
The Importance of Professionalism
Color Communication Works!

When **Holly Sallade** says that she's been in fashion for 25 years, people raise an eyebrow until they learn that she started her career in junior high school. She was a model, on the school board of models for two major Pittsburgh stores — Joseph Horne and Kaufman's — and even before she'd reached college age, had worked on in-store professional development promotions for *Glamour* and *Seventeen*. With this background it was natural that her college major was fashion merchandising.

She went on to teach fashion and professional development for a career school attuned to placing its graduates with the airlines and in the travel field. Her courses proved so popular that by the time she had become director of programs, 2,000 enrolled each year.

Several years ago she moved to the Washington, D.C., area, and in January, 1982, started *Color My Image, Ltd.* "My reason for doing this was the special kind of involvement you achieve. It is so rewarding to see someone walk out after a session and obviously be so much happier — both mentally and physically. Color communication really works. I know."

A Background in Fashion

To people starting out in the color/image consultant field, Holly Sallade stresses the importance of professionalism. She feels that a background in fashion, makeup, and color communication is important: "I worry about mistakes being made without this kind of knowledge."

She also stresses the importance of having a consultation area with white walls. "You can't get a true impression if other colors are reflecting off the wall. Once my assistant was doing consultation in someone's home and, in desperation, ended up in an empty bathtub! It was the *only* white-walled space available."

Another factor to remember is: "Don't underestimate the need for money 'ahead of you.' Find out what start-up expenses are involved, then project what else might be needed to maintain the success of your plan during a specified amount of time."

GLENDYS TINKLE:
Beauty for All Seasons
Most of Her Business Is From Word-of-Mouth

Having her colors done opened up a whole new career for **Glendys Tinkle** of Springfield, Virginia. A friend had been so enthusiastic about having *her* colors done that she went too. She not only liked the results, but decided to delve more deeply into the subject.

When she heard that the Idaho Falls, Idaho-headquartered "Beauty For All Seasons" (founded by **Norma** and **Wayne Virgin** and **Verla Ball**) was presenting an intensive weekend training seminar for potential consultants in her area, she signed up. Glendys Tinkle then became one of their more than 6,500 consultants in the United States, Canada, and other countries.

"Those classes were my greatest expense, but even so, they weren't nearly so costly as the expenses someone might have to budget to start up a different kind of business. I had to have the necessary color drapes and samples, but they were included with my class cost. I haven't really advertised — most of my business has come through word of mouth."

Working Out of Your Own Home

"I like the way a color/image consultant can work out of her home, and set her own schedule. It's an excellent occupation for someone with a family," says the mother of three.

To potential consultants, Tinkle emphasizes that "understanding of color is *so* important." She believes that it can be learned, but once one has this confidence, her feeling is that helping others becomes the main goal. "It's really satisfying to do something one enjoys *and* to see how good it makes others feel . . . to notice the reactions of the ones who watch as it happens!"

Victoria Eubanks, who is Beauty For All Seasons' Executive Director in the Washington, D.C., area, notes that independence and a neat appearance are among the qualifications her organization looks for in their consultants.

DEANNA RADELOFF:
Color Concept 7™
In Business Before She Knew It!

Dr. Deanna Radeloff first learned about color coding at the age of eight. "I was introduced to it when I was in the 4-H, and then used the color coding concept in connection with sewing in high school and college home economics classes."

Her interest in home economics led to several advanced degrees: a doctorate in education from the University of Michigan, a Masters in Clothing and Textiles from Ohio State University, and other degrees from the University of Toledo and Bowling Green State University, where she is on the faculty in Home Economics.

About four years ago Dr. Radeloff's friends started talking about how exciting the color concept ideas were. She recalls saying, "Oh, that's nothing new. We use color drapes in one of the classes at Bowling Green. Then I was asked, 'Can you color *me*?' 'Sure,' I answered, 'I'll borrow the drapes we have and let you see how they work on you.'

"Soon I was so busy color-draping people that I had to develop some draping bibs of my own. I was virtually in business before I knew it! To update myself in fashion — and to look at what was being done in the 'color business' in various parts of the country — I took additional training at Texas Women's University and Iowa State. After this, I told my husband that I felt I really should start my own company so that I could share what I had researched to accommodate a greater variation in skin tones for the color process. In August, 1982, I took the first steps."

Developing Your Own Color System

"When I first started color-draping, I had used a four-season approach, but quickly found that it didn't work on people such as my sister who is a 'Mosaic,' so I developed an individualized system."

Dr. Radeloff also noticed, among the 3,000 people whose colors she analyzed, that there were definite categories — not just in coloring, but in the type of questions they asked.

For example, most of the "Spicy" people loved their lavender eye shadow, but shouldn't have worn it because of the undertones in their skin. Although initially the most skeptical clients of color draping, they became the greatest advocates when they saw it in action.

As her color draping sessions and programs increased rapidly, Dr. Radeloff further perfected her system during a leave of absence from the university. She took the collected information and established *seven* color categories. In addition to "Spicy" and "Mosaic," the color harmonies she identified include "Misty Dawn," "Evening Glow," "Vivid Jewel," "Deep Jewel," and "Sunny." Each type was represented on a specially designed color wheel, and 85 color drapes were specifically silk-screened.

Now Dr. Radeloff certifies and trains her own Color Concept 7™ consultants. "When they are certified, they're on their own as independent business people. I don't receive royalties; they set their own rates (which for an individual consultation may vary from $45 in Columbus or Cleveland to $200 in San Francisco) and establish their own hours as 'Color Concept 7™' consultants."

MARY PENNISI:
A Texas-Size Success
From Kitchen Table to Spacious Studio

Mary Pennisi's Texas-size success as a color/image consultant shows in the way her business has grown from her kitchen table to the 1,800 square feet of her Color Studio, which has a neon rainbow as her colorful sign, where she employs a staff of five.

"Whenever I'm looking for staff people for The Color Studio, I want to be sure that they have a strong belief in what they are doing, and in the difference the right colors can make. The need for sensitivity and love of people is almost as important as a good eye for color, which is terribly important, and some background in art. We really deal with the psyche as well as the visual surface.

Dealing With Psyches and Visuals

People *should* come out happier. "Unless you give your new look a try, you'll never know. If for any reason the client isn't gathering *lots* of unsolicited compliments during the next two weeks, we want her to come back."

How did it all start? A New Yorker, Mary attended the Fashion Institute of Technology and Parsons School of Design. When she didn't feel bold enough at age 20 to storm Seventh Avenue, "I became a secretary and freelanced design and color concepts, and taught sewing and design in department stores. Then — to go back to square one — I had my colors done." Pennisi became an independent consultant when her family moved from New York to Texas.

"Freebies" That Became Referrals

"I wanted to make use of my new skills, so I joined a Newcomers' Club in Richardson, and gave a lecture. At first I was doing a fair number of freebie trade-offs . . . 'I'll do your colors if you . . . ,' but people expressed their satisfaction to the point where between 80 percent and 90 percent of my regular business was coming from referrals."

"I'd also follow up leads. When I heard that the homeowners' organization was looking for a speaker, I said, 'I'll do it!' Then someone told me that a local department store might be interested in putting on color classes. I talked to the director of public relations and she was interested — if I would be the one to place the ad, which would cost $250 at their special rate. I thought about it, and decided 'nothing invested, nothing gained.' It was a gamble, but turned out to be one that really paid off. Not only were those classes filled, but I received enough clients to keep me busy for 10 months. People were even flying in from Midland, Texas, in their private jets! These classes added greatly to my credibility so that my business really took off from that point."

LYNDA ROSENBERG:
A Visual Being
A Sense of Direction

Lynda Rosenberg feels that color/image consulting is just as competitive as other businesses.

"To be a success, one must always strive for perfection and total client satisfaction." Rosenberg's eye for detail encompasses everything from the business card ("find an excellent graphic designer for your card — stationery is *so* important!") to swatches ("I hired someone to cut them for me because every one of the 30 that my clients receive should be exactly right"). Her philosophy obviously works because her satisfied clients continue to build her reputation with numerous referrals.

"We all use our senses in different ways — being 'visual' is what's always been of prime importance to me." Her eye for the flattering undoubtedly has been influenced by her background. Having "grown up in fashion" (her mother had her own business) she became involved in fashion herself — learning every aspect, from buying to management, including styles, fabric, fit, and design.

After three-and-a-half years, she started her own business. At first it was built around the idea of "success dressing" and proper wardrobe coordination. Then in February 1982 she expanded into color analysis. "Clothing is a big investment. A woman (or man) can make costly mistakes if the color or the look doesn't work for the individual's personality and coloring. Knowing the right colors — 'this is me' gives a sense of direction that eliminates confusion when shopping. And the market *is* confusing, with so many stores, so many styles. By discovering *your* best colors, the ones that really complement *your* hair, skin and eyes, choosing clothing and makeup suddenly becomes *much* easier."

Cosmetics: Another Dimension

Rosenberg's clients clamored for a cosmetic line that would harmonize exactly with their "seasons," which led her to research a number of lines until she found one whose colors and quality suited her. Because the line she selected is sold only in hair salons, she has also become its area coordinator. "It's added another dimension to Executive Wardrobe Consultants."

Rosenberg is also a popular teacher in the Washington, D.C., area. Whenever one of her color classes is announced, it fills up so rapidly that additional classes have to be scheduled to take care of the overflow.

"It's All Very Fulfilling"

"The client interaction is highly personal. Everyone wants to look terrific, so it's such a pleasure when I can sense that the individual has been turned around and is now starting out with a sense of purpose and the kind of motivation that works toward achieving other goals, as well as improved appearance."

KAREN DAVIS:
Color Concepts
A Nudge From Fate

A nudge from fate gave **Karen Davis** her start as a color/image consultant. :"With a background in fashion I'd done a lot of wardrobe consultation in the retail business, and had been giving some thought to going out on my own. One day I attended a seminar on color — and won the door prize, which was the opportunity to have my own colors done! It seemed intended. After that, I read a lot — everything I could get my hands on that related to image and beauty, then studied with someone who specialized in training color consultants."

You Make The Decision How Much To Invest

"I found that the major expense is the training fee, but even that is relatively minor. You do need to buy your fabrics and palette — basically, that's it. *You* make the decision: how deeply do I want to go into it? Do I want to be low-key or high-profile?"

Davis feels that "Color Concepts" (the idea after which her business is named) frees a woman instead of restricting her. "Too many fall into the trap of thinking that they have to wear the *exact* tone. There's no magic to a certain shade. It can vary three degrees in either direction. You blend — you don't have to match exactly.

The Freedom

"I like the freedom of being a color/image consultant. It's really fun to take someone who isn't sure of herself, and show her that by wearing the right colors she will find that there *is* a great deal that's special about her, even if she doesn't have Elizabeth Taylor eyes! It's a great personal satisfaction.

"I couldn't do a good job unless I believed in the importance of color. That's why I love what I do, and I think that my clients sense my sincerity."

Davis has achieved one of her goals — making a success of her *"Color Concepts*"* and doing training herself. "Now I want to expand, build the business into areas that have not been tapped."

For newcomers to the field she stresses the importance of contacts, and the need to remember that doing colors is a one-time, not repeat, business. "It's important to be flexible. Test to make sure you aren't going into an area where the color market is already crowded. Color/image consultation has become so accessible that you may be surprised to find color consultants already established in what you might have considered a remote village. No wonder the field is growing so fast — it really is a fascinating profession!"

*The color theory here is *not* that of ColorConcept 7.

CLARE MILLER:
The Five Faces of Woman
"My Mother Made Me!"

Today **Clare Miller** is internationally known as a makeup artist although her "Five Faces of Woman" is located in the Dallas area. And of all the consultants with whom we have spoken, she has the most unusual reason for embarking on a consultant career. "My mother made me!"

When she was a teenager, Miller suffered badly from acne. Not only were eight long years of visits to dermatologists, courses of antibiotics, and other treatments futile, she found that the extensive use of antibiotics was destroying her health. The frustration of those years of feeling less than attractive and secure made her determined either to become beautiful or know the reason why!

Her mother began using a natural organic cosmetic, which helped beautify her skin, and decided that it would help her daughter too. "Amazingly, it did! In her enthusiasm for the results of those products, Mother began to sell them. She carved out such a superior sales career that she soon needed a manager reporting to her. Guess to whom she turned!"

By this time Miller, a Katharine Gibbs graduate, was already successfully pursuing another career. In order to force her to begin, even part-time, her mother made appointments with clients in her name!

Hooked on the Cinderella Experience

"I, of course, was soon hooked by the thrill of the Cinderella experience . . . watching a woman improve her life as you assist in her beauty and image metamorphosis. Instead of initially attending cosmetology school — getting either a CDS (Cosmetic Demonstrator Specialist) license or a license to do facials, and then progressing to makeup artist, I advanced in nearly the reverse order. Within a few years, I was working in the beauty industry exclusively, and rose to become the youngest chairman of the board in the history of my corporation. In 1979, she received an "Award d'Elegance" in Paris. Today she averages 500 speaking engagements annually in addition to her client practice and is a favorite subject for media interviews.

Miller has noticed certain characteristics which seem to be shared by the best makeup consultants: an artistic bent or flair, a firm foundation in skin care/makeup applications, and an understanding of total "style" or image. The person should be able to see the potential in the new client, and be able to teach her how to achieve the effects the artist has created. The very nature of consulting requires self-motivation, self-discipline. And, she maintains, "There's no replacement for experience in this business!"

What You Can Do

1. Remember you're "on" at all times . . . be sure to keep your own appearance neat and up-to-date.

2. Make sure you keep "money ahead of you" for your operation . . . to allow for "fast times and feast times."

3. See the potential in every new client.

4. Remind your clients that they may need a little time to adjust to their new looks.

5. Learn more about skin care and makeup application.

6. Study the "go-together principles" of makeup and clothing colors.

Chapter 8

The Fashion Consultants: Personal Shoppers

While color is important to fashion consultants, they generally consider it just one element of the total picture. As a specialty career, the title of "fashion consultant" has been around much longer than that of "color advisor." But how it has changed in the last 15 or 20 years!

In the past, fashion consultants found their prime customers among the brides who were trousseau-collecting, teenagers whose parents didn't want them to go off to college without a complete wardrobe, and the very wealthy.

All this has changed — drastically. As consultant **Brenda York** explains it:

"People today don't have as much time to be shopper-browsers as they did in the past. They're also much more aware of the impact the right image can have when it comes time for promotions or other 'goodies' in life."

The growth in the fashion/image consultant field can be attributed to this interest. New kinds of fashion experts are emerging . . . and they are very articulate when they speak out on what it takes to make it successfully now and in the future.

EMILY CHO:
Image Innovator
Paving the Way

The person many credit with being the actual founder of the personal fashion consulting industry is **Emily Cho.**When she started her own business, "New Image,"in 1970, she brought to it what could well be considered a Triple Crown of fashion credentials: buyer for Bloomingdale's, editor,*Seventeen* and Vogue-Butterick, booking agent for the Ford Model Agency.

Cho sensed the need for this service because clothing was becoming increasingly expensive and trends increasingly confusing. When the personal insecurities that beset people are added, it's clear that a person who knows fashion and is interested in making sure her clients look their best can become a big success.

By 1976 New Image had become so well known that the *New York Times* assigned a reporter to accompany Emily and a client on their six-hour shopping expedition. The conclusion: an image consultant had to be a dynamic combination of fashion advisor, confidant, and (sometimes) firm friend who would steer the client away from unwise budget choices.

Introducing a Low-cost Wardrobe Plan

Since then, Cho's fame has continued to grow as a consultant, and as the author of *Looking Terrific: Express Yourself Through the*

Language of Clothing (Putnam, 1978) and *Looking, Working, Living Terrific 24 Hours a Day* (Putnam, 1982). But she's done even more! Because of her concern about women who wanted to avail themselves of New Image advice but might not be able to afford it, she turned to the computer for help. By answering a $25 computerized questionnaire, recipients can now get an individualized wardrobe plan; this innovation has been so popular that Cho has received more than 5,000 responses.

Also, following a decade of requests, she has recently started offering a two-day course in the image business for consultants and their assistants.

While in Washington recently, Cho told the *Washington Post* that the image business is thriving for the same basic reasons that people go to image-makers: "It helps them gain confidence, beat the competition, ease the pressure, and look up-to-the-minute in yesterday's clothes."

BRENDA YORK:
The American Society of Fashion and Image Consultants
From Teacher to Sales Rep

Before she became an image consultant six years ago, **Brenda York** had taught fashion merchandising and modeling, and was a special representative for Estee Lauder. "Atlanta was my base, but I actually worked in New York, Los Angeles, Miami, and every major area of the country. I got a good feel for what was going on geographically with a variety of major retailers.

"It was a tremendous experience because the involvement was with the total picture of fashion. The colors of makeup have an effect on the overall image, so I did a number of TV interview shows as well, explaining current trends in cosmetics and color. Then, when my son was born, I didn't want the extensive travel, and wondered how I could continue doing interesting work. My decision was to become a fashion/image consultant, and I built my reputation through teaching and word-of-mouth referrals."

Look Ahead to Where You'll Be Going

Through her work with individuals and corporate clients, York has established a 30-hour course known as the Academy of Fashion and Image Consulting to assist prospective consultants. "People have to have the right kind of training to establish their credentials. You can't charge $45 to $75 per hour just because you 'have good taste and enjoy shopping.' I want them to define their objectives, be aware of strengths and weaknesses, and look ahead to know where they will be going. They need a high level of energy, good discipline, and organization."

Because of her concern with the level of professionalism clients should be able to count on from consultants, she recently did extensive research and founded the American Society of Fashion and Image Consultants. From her McLean, Virginia base, York says, "I knew of the image interest in the metropolitan area, but was delighted with the nationwide responses I received after a story ran in the *Washington Post*. There are lots of us who share this concern . . . a primary purpose of which is to develop more universal certification or accreditation, plus establishing a 'network' for consultants."

HELEN MOODY:
The Tastemaker of Any Group
"Women Want Clothes that Make Them Special"

"While doing personal shopping I learned a secret — why those Diane von Furstenberg wrap dresses were such a phenomenal success! The comfortable fabric reminded women of the cozy baby outfits their mothers had put them in, and that wide sash was like an extra hug," recalls **Helen Moody.**

"Women want clothes that make them feel special. That's why they need a good wardrobe consultant because they frequently are most vulnerable when they go shopping in a store where some salesperson may or may not really place their interests first."

Freelance fashion consultant Moody is very much as she describes her favorite clients: "A free spirit who makes a contribution."

Recently, at a wedding, a former teacher came up to her and said, "I always knew that you'd end up in fashion one way or another ever since I saw you as a four-year-old who wanted to re-arrange Mary's halo in the Christmas pageant!"

Harnessing the Excitement

Helen grew up in a house with a mirrored hallway, and a grandmother who taught her to look in the mirrors to see what fashion statement her clothes were making. She credits her grandmother as her image-maker, harnessing the excitement in her. "As a three-year-old I was taken shopping and headed straight for bright red taffeta. Grandmother never criticized my taste outright, she harnessed it and protected me without taking away my freedom. Even then she said, 'Why, that's very nice, dear,' but also turned to the salesperson and added softly, 'You DO have that in velvet?' "

By the time Helen Moody was 14, she was considered the tastemaker of her group . . . mothers insisted their daughters take her along when they set forth with family charge cards for shopping expeditions."I'd say, 'You *know* your mother won't let a 14-year-old keep a red strapless that's slit to the navel!', and they'd listen to me!"

Longing for a Job with Greater Freedom

When Moody finished school and was ready for a career, she abandoned a childhood dream of becoming a lady riverboat gambler for something more serious — public relations at the American Red Cross. She longed for a job with greater freedom, however, and a friend who was managing the Saks Fifth Avenue branch in Chevy Chase, Maryland, offered her one — part modeling, part personal shopper. "He was very good at spotting people he thought would bring something positive to the store whether they had a fashion background or not.

"During the one-and-a-half year I was there I covered that store like a whirlwind! None of my customers left until I felt that every detail, every accessory, was perfect. For example, if a customer bought a see-through dress, our next stop would be the lingerie department in case she didn't have the right underwear for such a dress!"

About the same time that new management arrived, Moody had to have an operation, which took her out of circulation for several months. The combination of events ended her Saks connection, but didn't discourage her customers! They continued to call the store and say, "I *know* you don't give out employees' phone numbers, but will you contact Helen Moody and ask her to call me." One even went so far as to respond to Moody's explanation that her doctor wouldn't let her dash around for some time with the offer: "You just sit down in the store — I'll dash around! What I want is to have you tell me what I should buy!" After that, she started freelancing full-time, one of the first personal shoppers to have such a following.

MARY B. FIEDOREK:
The Executive's Executive
Polishing the Business Image

Mary B. Fiedorek applied her knowledge of fashion so successfully that by the time she was in her mid-twenties she was buyer of better suits, coats, and dresses at Bergdorf Goodman. At first she considered the effectiveness of her choices, but not necessarily their practicality for the business world. She couldn't understand why her friends in more conservative professions might not feel secure enough to wear whatever pleased them on their jobs. Gradually, however, she saw that there was a need for an "executive style."

Researching the Market

Fiedorek also began to see this need as something that might inspire an entire store. Before she turned her dream into actuality, she spent two years working with a market research firm to ensure that such a store would provide what the executive woman really wanted, in terms of service as well as fashion. Through focus-group interviews with women who were making annual salaries of $25,000 or more, she discovered that they had very specific clothing priorities which had more to do with judgment than style.

Then, when she was 28, she and her financial partner opened "Streets & Co." in March,1980, on New York's busy West Side. They selected the unusual name in order to avoid one that might turn into an outdated catch phrase. With this name they were able to salute a wide variety of business action areas — from New York's Wall Street to Washington's K Street lawyers' canyon, and all the Main Streets across the country.

The Unique Result

Mary is proud that hers became the first free-standing store designed to fit all the qualifications set forth by the executive women who had been interviewed — including more convenient shopping hours, a full-time tailor, and messenger delivery service. Before the opening, as a final step, she had 25 of her survey respondents come in and removed any designs they disliked from her stock! Not surprisingly, the garment that continues to be most in demand is the suit. When the *New York Times* wrote about this store after the opening, the article described Fiedorek as a tall, slender woman who could wear any style, but who tended to choose the clothes she sold because "I'm a working woman too — I find this kind of conservative dress does make my life easier."

Branching Out

Today Mary Fiedorek's "Executive Style" concept has become so popular it has inspired a book about the principles: *Executive Style. Looking It. Living It.* "Streets & Co." is doing extremely well too. In the fall of 1983, Mary opened her first branch — on New York's East Side, and planned to follow it with a location in Midtown Manhattan. After that? New "Streets & Co." operations in other metropolitan cities; she hopes to open one a year.

What advice does Mary Fiedorek have for a prospective fashion consultant? "A lot of people look askance at consultants because they aren't sure what the title entails. I feel that it's a 'must' to work in a major store for several years. It takes time to sense the changing seasons and trends, to get a sense of the fashion excitement this provides . . . fashion excitment you might miss in a very small store."

RUTHANNE OLDS:
Image on a Grand Scale
Opportunities for Specializing

One of the most exciting aspects of the image-consultant field is the great variety of opportunities it offers for specialization. Californian **Ruthanne Olds** makes a point of showing women how to overcome "fatphobia," and be attractive and successful even if they aren't a size 10 or smaller. As a person who knows what it's like to look for larger-size fashions, she can empathize with clients who want something more becoming than "blob" clothes.

"After college, while working in public relations for a chain of fabric stores, I became increasingly aware of the way a segment of the market was being overlooked by the majority of designers." She found that part of the blame for this should be shared by the potential customers.

"When I would speak before groups, I'd get clients, but they weren't the ones I wanted — they were thin! Too many of the larger-size women wouldn't admit that theirs was anything except a 'temporary body' . . . were just waiting for the magic day when their perfect size-nine shape would appear. In the meantime they weren't concentrating on making the best of themselves *right now.*"

Mapping It All Out On Paper

"I knew it would take time to reach these people, but I'd been a home-ec major and learned the way office management techniques could be applied to the home. I decided to reverse this idea and reapply them to business — mine! The first thing I did when I decided to become an image consultant was to map everything out on paper.

I feel that you can avoid a lot of problems this way. Something that bothers me about a number of women starting their own businesses is the tendency to be unprofessional about details. If you can't make it on paper, you can't make it in the real world."

To anyone starting out as an image consultant, whether in color, fashion, or public image, Olds' first piece of advice is, "Always be totally pulled together yourself. Have that immaculate, well-groomed appearance that shows you know you are your own best product."

Finally, she adds, "if you should happen to move from a large city to a small town, take the time to develop a sense of what's important in that particular community. Don't try to impose one area's set of fashion standards on another place until you find out if they are appropriate for the new location's 'big events.' "

CHARLES HIX:
From Fiction To Fashion
Delivering the Male

Sometimes *not* getting the job you want can lead to accomplishments you never planned. That's what happened to **Charles Hix** after his arrival in New York in 1963. He'd just been graduated from the University of Michigan, where he received a prestigious literary prize, and was sure that the publishing world was waiting for him. It wasn't, and he found himself selling books instead of writing them.

After several years as paperback manager for Doubleday, he became a reporter on *Home Furnishings Daily*. There he advanced to floor-covering editor before leaving for a job in public relations.

Developing a Reputation

This was not his favorite kind of writing so he "just happened" to get into magazine work. Then, he told *Contemporary Authors*,[4]

"I was lucky — developed a reputation as an expert in covering men's grooming and fashion."

From this reputation came an editor's offer. Why not write a book about his field of expertise? He did, and *Looking Good* became the first book totally dedicated to men's grooming to be listed as a *New York Times* best-seller. Although Hix hopes to be remembered for the fiction he will write during his lifetime, he is currently associated with the field of men's image. He has also written *Dressing Right: A Guide for Men* and columns on "Imaging" and "Looking Good," and conducted seminars on men's fashion.

Because men are increasingly aware that "Looking Good" is important, the numbers of those who will be seeking expert advice from image consultants are likely to grow rapidly.

VERDALE BENJAMIN:
Total Image Associates
Incorporating Dress in Corporate Finesse

When **Verdale Benjamin** started conducting seminars on career development about eight years ago, she didn't realize that a career as an image consultant would be an outgrowth. "The seminars focused on job-hunting strategies for women. Gradually a new need emerged — what to wear for interviews and appropriate attire for work. Based on my own experience and that of others, I gradually incorporated attire into these seminars. Because of my background in research, I was able to obtain materials that others had since forgotten . . . books by **Mary Kefgen, Charleszine Spears,** and **Edith Head** were my bibles."

A Black Woman:
Sensitivity to Specific Needs

Today Benjamin is president of Total Image Associates, an organization that works with many groups. As a black woman, she has been particularly sensitive to that group's specific needs. "Because of the unavailability of 'ethnic' goods for black women 20 years ago, many of us grew up trying to emulate the images shown on TV. In other words, we tried to be something other than what we were. I show my clients how to be like themselves and be proud of it, but I don't limit my consultancy to black women. Some of the workshops and seminars I conduct for men and women of all ages and sizes include: Style Elements: Wardrobing for Men; Making it Big (women sized 16 and over); Fine, Fabulous and Over Forty; and Women Should Mind Their Own Their Own Business (for women contemplating business ownership)."

People-Oriented and People-Propelled

While a sense of fashion (and appropriate fashion) is essential, Benjamin considers certain qualities of character even more crucial for someone wanting to specialize as she has: *"Perseverance* . . . don't take 'no' as a personal rejection. *Self-motivation, leadership, and initiative* . . . be ready to take charge, stay in control of the situation. Be people-oriented; people-propelled."

Establishing Your Credentials

What advice does she have for those who've taken the plunge and are ready to start their new career? "From the outset establish your credentials and credibility. Read everything you can on the subject — successful business ownership, PMA, fashion merchandising, fashion careers, and the consultant industry in particular. Join visible organizations; speak up; organize some worthwhile project to give yourself visibility. Be the very best you can be."

Benjamin credits her success to three factors: "First and foremost in my life is the Creator. All my ideas, enthusiasm, and energy emanate from Him. Second, people. One of my greatest joys is knowing that

I have had a positive impact on someone else's life. The third is hard work and perseverance; thinking, being, acting creatively in the face of adverse economic conditions. I try to remain versatile. Don't stop with Plan A — always be ready 'to go into Plan B.' "

NANCY THOMPSON:
Image Awareness
Focusing on the First 20 Seconds

Nancy Ames Thompson of Image Awareness focuses on the corporate area, working particularly with corporations that recognize how important 20-second first impressions can be, and want the lasting impression to be one of confidence and credibility.

Thompson, whose interest in riding, hunting, and sailing nurtured an appreciation of good tailoring, good quality, and appropriate garb at a young age, went straight from school to the fabric department of *Vogue* Magazine. She later became secretary/assistant to Vogue's famed fashion editor, **Polly Mellon.** "Polly is one of the *great* 'eyes' . . . her *Vogue* sittings show it today as they did in the late 1960's when I was at the magazine."

For Thompson, assisting Mellon and going on photographic assignments provided advanced fashion training. "It really was hands-on training. One had to have a real understanding of proper fit and proportion when the models with whom we worked were far taller than average. The exotic look and background might make the photograph more intriguing, but the fashion had to fit to make the clothes look right."

Presenting a Better-Proportioned Look

After four years with *Vogue*, Thompson went to *Glamour* as model editor, which sharpened her appreciation of correct proportioning even more. "I still think that way. Someone else might see a really beautiful woman and say, 'What a knockout!' I'd probably think, 'no, she isn't . . . her legs are too short!' There are, of course, ways to present a better proportioned look,"

Thompson, while *Glamour's* Accessories Editor, deserted the fashion world for the nation's capital when a political campaign of national importance came up. Although her candidate lost, she stayed on in Washington to found "Image Awareness" in 1977.

 "Too many women feel that no one ever taught them how to dress. As children, it was always Mommy who made the decisions, and during the teen years it seemed important to be a clone of your friends. Then, as grown-up professionals, it often becomes "what do I do now!' "

"I knew I could communicate the principles they needed to apply: the necessity for good proportion, fit, color, fabric, and appropriate style. I knew that it was a learning process like any other, that people could be taught to recognize what to look for to flatter them individually — such as where a jacket should hit on the body, and what colors would create an impression some might call the 'power look.' "

Working in the Trenches of the Fashion Industry

To become a successful image consultant, Thompson believes that an innate fashion sense is a "must." "But," she adds, "I don't think it's enough to just have the fabled 'eye' . . . there should be training so there is professional backing — perhaps in a school such as Parsons School of Design for a couple of years, or work in the trenches of the fashion industry.

"The training will also sharpen the ability to look at a person from many perspectives, and help the consultant avoid making snap decisions about the client until she has acquired a variety of information about the person. There are all kinds of ways you can help the client look better."

"People do react to the way the individual sees her or himself. If the consultant is able to make this person be happier about appearance, the individual will draw happier reactions."

JANET WALLACH:
Working Wardrobe
Putting the Pieces Together

Janet Wallach is a person who knows how to put the pieces together — in fashion, career, and lifestyle, and in her book, *Working Wardrobe*, shows others how to take advantage of what *Modern Bride* referred to as the "new fashion math."

While at New York University, where she majored in writing, she was offered a summer job running a showroom on Seventh Avenue. "I liked it so much that I continued working full-time while I was in college; after graduation and several years on Seventh Avenue, I became a designer for the sportswear house of Herman Geist."

She later moved to Washington where she entered the retail side of the fashion picture, first as a fashion coordinator for Woodward & Lothrop, then fashion merchandising director at Garfinckel's. "I developed my 'Capsule Concept' from several experiences in different fashion situations. First, as a sportswear designer, I'd develop a group of separates based around two colors so that one jacket might go with a variety of other pieces and the skirts or pants would coordinate with different tops. Later I traveled a great deal and needed to pack a lot of looks in one suitcase. When you arrive in Europe and discover that all the porters are on strike, you quickly learn not to take any more than you can manage carrying yourself! In doing seminars for the store, I saw how interested women were in having an easy, affordable way to build a good wardrobe that would really work."

Specializing in Groups

Wallach specializes in group, rather than individual, presentations. She believes that potential consultants need a good sense of their own style, and a highly developed flair for clothes. She advises them to study fashion to acquire the "educated eye" that can see what's flattering, how to combine new purchases with items in the existing wardrobe, and sense multi-possibilities so that the total effect is very much the right one. Also essential: an understanding of others' needs, in terms of their lifestyles, their work, fashion — and the real world!

CINDY HARSLEY:
The "Persnickety" Shopper
'This Is What You Should Do'

New Yorker **Cindy Harsley** studied at the Textile & Design School (later named after Charles Evan Hughes), then attended the Fashion Institute of Technology. Her first "garment district" job was with a manufacturer of ladies' fur-trimmed coats, but she broadened her fashion training when she became a stylist for the large photographic studio headed by **Constantin Joffe**, one of *Vogue's* original photographers, where they did everything from introduce "glamour in the shower" for Dial soap to fashion layouts for *Mademoiselle.*

After a stint at *Vogue*, she decided to join her fiance in Washington. *Vogue's* editor, **Diana Vreeland**, recommended her to **Katharine Graham,** owner of *The Washington Post*, where she started a new job working on the fashion page.

"It was at the *Post* that I moved in the direction of becoming a fashion/image consultant. Many of the women reporters said that they didn't have time to find 'a dress I can just throw on in the ladies' room, then wear for a variety of occasions.' I started personal shopping for the kind of basics that could be varied with different accessories. They were so pleased that they said, 'This is what you should do!' I decided they were right since I enjoyed doing it so much, so I became a full-time consultant about 10 years ago."

You Have to Care about People

Although Harsley's clients include a number of fashion-conscious black women, she says that skin color is far from the first consideration when she makes selections. "I look at the person from the standpoint of her personality and job — then think what colors are good for the skin.

"You have to care about people if you want to be in this field, but there are other characteristics you need as well to become a fashion/image consultant. One is a definite fashion sense — and understanding fashion in a broad way. Some people do a great job of dressing tall, thin women, but are not able to work with any other body type. You have to be open-minded, to make sure your selections will be the ones that flatter the *individual*. I spend a lot of time in research so that I can know not only which designers specialize in certain types, but who's got what now, and where. Another important characteristic is patience."

With her new clients, Harsley takes extra time to see what the client likes and what works for her. "Sometimes the person may be a little undecided and say something such as 'I *think* I like that, but I'm not sure.' In other cases the client may be locked into incorrect fashion ideas, but in all cases I have to guide them to what *is* actually better for them. It's so satisfying when they come back and tell me how great people have said they look. Of course, they believe me while I'm working with them, but what really builds their confidence in me is when they hear it from others. Whether it's four or five years later or the next day, it's very pleasing to have a client tell the consultant, 'that outfit you chose for me — it really worked out!' "

Insiders' Perspectives

What about a "store-side perspective"? You *can* be a fashion consultant without being a freelancer. Check the leading stores in your area. A number of them will probably have a person with this title, or a similar one. Although it may not be designated officially, it's very likely that management hires someone who makes this her speciality.

GERRY KENDALL:
Advice from a Large Specialty Store
Instinct is not Enough

Austrian-born **Gerry Kendall** moved from modeling into the fashion consultant field. "Fashion has been very good to me in giving me the freedom to accomodate family and other personal priorities. Most of the consultants I know, freelancers as well as staff people in other stores, share this 'store' background . . . either from selling, buying, or some other phase of merchandising.

Kendall, now a fashion consultant for Garfinckels, in Washington, D.C., says,"You may have an inborn instinct, but you only make it rough on yourself if you don't learn to cope with a lot of limitations. By working in a store you get exposure to merchandise availability, know the current market, understand delivery timing and appreciate seasonal specials. You also get more exposure to a wide variety of customer concerns. It's important that the consultant have a number of interests, a rounded background so that she can answer her clients' questions about what's appropriate to wear for a variety of events and help them achieve the kind of good wardrobes that provide a sense of fashion security.

"Wardrobes should be well-balanced, able to fit into most situations except for the really unexpected. Unless it's a conference being held on short notice in an entirely different climate, or dinner at the White House, you really should never have to cry, 'I don't have a thing to wear!'

"Two 'secrets' can prevent this, and they are easy to apply: planning and evolvement." For her clients, Kendall seeks the kind of selections the purchaser can count on wearing and enjoying for several seasons.

HARRIET KASSMAN:
Advice from a Boutique
Boutique Mystique

What about the boutique or specialty store owner who might be hiring a fashion consultant to work in his or her establishment? What qualities would they look for?

Harriet Kassman, owner of the successful specialty store which bears her name, says, "The person should have an 'eye' for fashion as well as an interest in the field, really care about people, and have an air of authority that will lend weight to her recommendations."

"Personal service is especially important in the specialty store, since the emphasis is on wanting the customer to be happy to have a reason for buying . . . not to feel that shopping is just a chore she must do. We find out about our customers — what their lifestyles are, where they go, what they do — it's all important when we're helping them build the appropriate image."

"We tell our staff that it's important to remember that bodies aren't ready-made even if the clothes are. Making sure that her selection fits her properly determines about 50 percent of the way the customer-client looks."

Because most women today have some kind of career, part-time or full-time, fashion demands are different from what they were in the past. Those who go on from a full day on the job require a special kind of simplicity that looks well in a variety of situations.

For those entering the fashion image-making field, Kassman has several bits of advice:"Keep an open mind . . . you should be aware of the constant need to explore different directions, but *not* be out for instant fashion revolution in a client's wardrobe. Remember that fashion is really an evolutionary process . . . and know your area. For some places a very dramatic effect might be completely appropriate, in other more conservative cities, it would look wild rather than indicate a flair for fashion."

Kassman also is very realistic about entry-level jobs in the fashion field. "Beginners usually come in as salespeople, or possibly glorified helpers in executive training. However, there's definitely an encouraging note. Anyone who has real talent gets picked up very quickly . . . probably more so in the fashion business than anywhere else!"

JOHN MOLLOY:
The Wardrobe Engineer
Dressing Millions for Success

Whether they love the formula or hate its "uniform" restrictiveness, nearly everyone knows who is responsible for the term "dress for success"™ becoming a fashion philosophy. He is **John Molloy,** who would rather be thought of as a "wardrobe engineer" than an image consultant, although he has consulted for corporations from General Motors to U. S. Steel.

A little over 20 years ago Molloy kept busy as a young English teacher in a Connecticut prep school. As much as he loved his work, the pay was so miserable he felt he couldn't continue. The school's owner was sympathetic. Although it wasn't possible to give him a raise, he understood the problem and offered to find a part-time job.

Researching and Experimenting

A summer project turned up. A group of teachers had received a government grant to do remedial teaching and general research in education. As his project Molloy chose the effects of clothing on learning. He now admits that he was a little frightened when his project was accepted. He didn't consider any of the teachers — including himself — as qualified researchers at the time, but he needed the money. He immediately set out for the library to read everything he could find on the subject of research.

When he felt he had learned enough about research methods, he conducted his experiments, which proved that the clothing worn by teachers actually did affect the attitudes of the pupils. Just at the point of his discovery, the project ran out of funding!

But this didn't stop him. "Hooked" by the implications, Molloy started taking courses and did additional research on his own. When he presented the completed report, another blow fell. He was told that even if his findings were valid, they wouldn't know what to do with them!

Temporarily crushed, he returned to teaching, then found a Christmastime job at a prestigious Fifth Avenue store, selling men's clothing. He quickly built up a following among lawyers. One day he responded to the comment, "This is my sincere suit!" with "No, it's not!" One partner believed in grey for "sincerity," the other in blue, and Molloy told them "one of you has to be wrong!" They liked his research approach, and started bringing in other members of the firm in a group. His boss wasn't too thrilled with the response, since others weren't getting the commissions he was pulling in . . . so actually tried to put his order on someone else's book. That did it, and Mr. Molloy and his clients took their business to another store!

Valuable Feedback from Clients

His clients became increasingly interested in Molloy's research and his service. They hired him, and it really did become a case of "build a better mousetrap." The lawyers told the politicians, the politicians told others, and his list of clients grew and grew.

Molloy's organization now works with more than 100 major corporate organization clients. "We've grown like Topsy."

Sharing His Knowledge

After years of working with clients and seeing how effective the concepts were proving, he wrote *Dress for Success*, followed two years later by *The Woman's Dress for Success Book*. He emphasizes that his findings are based on research rather than on his own opinion, and has a self-deprecating story to explain. "When I first started out, I purchased twelve suits, then decided that my selections had been influenced by my lower middle-class background, and were wrong. I gave away eight of them — would have made it ten if I could have afforded it then!" And, he adds, "I immediately discarded my black raincoat!"

He feels that clothes should be thought of as tools . . . that dressing is a matter of conditioning to the socio-economic background rather than just intending to give aesthetic pleasure. "Unfortunately some consultants who set themselves up as corporate advisors are lightweights who've never really known the corporate world and give advice that can be disastrously counterproductive. I don't care who the consultant is, *always* ask the person 'where did you get your information?

Being an image consultant is a wonderful field for young people. When our Dress for Success, Inc.™ organization hires, we look for those who have a master's in psychology, then give them a written and oral test . . . as well as a color test. It's amazing how many people *are* color blind to blue and green, or its variations. In addition we want people who are *not* emotionally involved with clothing. It's not just for young people . . . most recently we've been hiring retired executives who understand the needs of other executives."

Molloy can appreciate the tremendous opportunities in a field he can't help but think of as "my baby." In addition to his fast-growing organization that has grown so fast he now finds himself, the president, more involved with public relations-type activities than having time for doing consultation himself, he gives a number of speeches (a recent one in California attracted an audience of 2,000, with women accounting for two-thirds of this corporate interest). He continues to get a great deal of reader response to his books, enjoys seeing a number of his clients on best-dressed lists, but prefers keeping a low profile about being their advisor, and will soon be seeing the well-known "dress for success" words on lines of clothing for men and women.

Obviously a lot has changed since the early 60's! A list of accomplishments like this provide an impressive indication of what study, applied intelligence, and hard work can accomplish.

What You Can Do

1. Put it on paper . . . map things out ahead of time before you do something in reality to have a better idea of whether or not it will work.

2. If moving to a new area, check out its fashion standards before you make specific client suggestions.

3. Get fashion training . . . establish your credentials.

4. Make sure of proper fit.

5. Remember the secret of any good wardrobe is planning *and* evolvement (be willing to work with what the client has rather than taking the easy route of starting brand-new).

6 Act creatively so if for any reason your first plan of action doesn't work the way you want it to, you can have a "Plan B" available.

Chapter 9

Public Image & Speech Consultants

Making It in the Public Eye

Everything relates. Color is linked to fashion. Fashion choices affect the way you look, as well as the way you feel. Public-image consultants consider these elements, but generally deal with the *total* image — the way their clients look, sound, and present themselves.

These consultants build client confidence in dealing with hostile media or audiences. They coach them on speaking techniques and styles and show them how to be at ease in front of a camera or behind a lectern.

Since public image encompasses content as well as appearance and speaking style, speechwriters and public relations/public affairs experts often consult with the image people who coach others.

LOU HAMPTON:
Communications Strategies
Skills, Teaching Ability, Synthesizing, Tact

Interested in becoming a public/image consultant? **Lou Hampton**, president of Hampton Communications Strategies, comments that you should have:

"*Skills* that you can share with others. *Teaching ability* , which may be as important as having the skill itself. Consider sports, and the analytically minded coaches who bring out the best in their players. A flair for *synthesizing* — finding what's useful in a clutter of material that hasn't been pulled together tightly. *Tact* in a variety of situations. Be a good *money manager*. If you concentrate on thinking of yourself as a small business, you'll keep an eye on the cash flow, and be managing money well."

Dreamed of Becoming a Radio Announcer

When he was a small child, Hampton dreamed of becoming a radio announcer. Then, as a ninth grader, "I had a teacher who was really fantastic . . . instilled in the class such an appreciation for good writing and reading that my interests broadened." Practicality overrode his college desire to become a professional actor, and he became a teacher in a Washington, D.C.-area prep school. He did, however, continue acting in suburban productions.

Through contacts with his pupils' parents, he began doing freelance writing, sales and convention presentations, speeches, and radio spots. Business grew, and Hampton left teaching to join the American Learning Society as their Director of Marketing until the 1974 recession hit the audio-visual market. Re-joining the education world for a year as a prep school assistant headmaster convinced him that his main interest was more in communications so, "in 1976, I went to New York and took advanced training from Dorothy Sarnoff, a leading speech and image consultant."

Making the Most of Uniqueness

When Hampton returned to Washington and opened his own business, he was the only full-time person in the field in D.C. who was not connected with a university or New York firm. "All this has changed considerably since then!"

As senior vice president of Hampton Bates & Associates, he taught government and corporate clients how to deal with the media. He trained them to communicate effectively on TV, radio, and in print, in speeches and seminars, and to develop the art of listening effectively.

When he became president of Hampton Communication Strategies in 1983, he broadened his communications programs even more.

"I especially like working with individual clients — teaching them how to make the most of their uniqueness. When I set out to find this quality, I strip away the negative distractions so the focus can be on the positive. The exact right polka dot for a tie isn't going to count as much as the person's having good substance. Since I'm interested in results, I'll give the client an extra session if I feel they've done their part, but haven't quite gotten it. I want *them* to succeed!"

Strategizing for Problem Solving

"I enjoy teaching classes too, but the thing I find most intriguing is strategizing for problem-solving. We may work with teams of people, use cassettes for reinforcement, try out different strategies until the results appear . . . and the results can be very measurable, perhaps the landing of a big government contract, or a dramatic upturn in closing sales. With a number of organizations, I'm on retainer . . . come in when there is a new person to train or a problem or program comes up that requires special strategies."

"While Washington, D.C. is certainly a key 'media market,' there are opportunities for public/image consultants in *many* smaller cities."

JAMES G. GRAY, JR.:
Projecting a Professional Image
The Winning Image: Unspoken Symbols

Several years ago at American University's Communications School, professor **James G. Gray, Jr.** created a course in ways to create and project a professional image. It proved so successful that he turned it into seminars for the university's Department of Continuing Education, began offering personal coaching with his own "Media Impact" business, and published a book on *The Winning Image* (American Management Association, 1982.).

"I've been amazed at the level of the people who attend the seminars and come for special coaching. They're *not* newcomers, but well-established professionals. Here in the Washington area I see a great number of government relations experts and lawyers. They know how important it is to make the very best of one's presentation skills when facing critical audiences."

"**Albert Mehrabian** approximates that from 50 percent to 70 percent of the impact comes from the non-verbal presentation. I'd go even further, say 85 percent, with 15 percent for the spoken message. Take, for example, a news program, which, in 20½ minutes, covers the events of the world, the entire reality. There's no question that a large part of image comes from unspoken signals."

His advice to potential image consultants: "The best formula to establish is to make sure you *always* offer a quality presentation so that your clients walk away feeling that have learned something worthwhile. Building this kind of advertising will help you build outward from that core."

LILLIAN BROWN:
Media Image Consultant
Once a P.T.A. Mother

Lillian Brown has been a highly successful freelance media/image consultant for the past seven years.

She had taught at Ohio State University before her family moved to Virginia. "With three small children to support, I was a typical P.T.A. mother, and chairman of the Arlington County Speech service committee. Arlington County schools were offered free TV time, but weren't too interested in taking it because they didn't have any material. I suggested doing a Virginia history — as seen through the eyes of the children who had lived in the historic mansions. It went over so well that the National Council of Churches became interested in a series on the churches of the presidents."

One thing led to another, and Brown went to CBS 25 years ago. She also became a radio/TV producer for American University and George Washington University — (each for a stint of 10 years), and began coaching public figures and working at the Voice of America.

"When I started coaching people for television appearances, I became quite conscious of the effects of the camera lenses and the lighting. I spoke at length with the technicians and experts to pick up more inside knowledge. You have to be alert to learning opportunities at all times because you're in the kind of environment where if you don't learn you're likely to lose out."

Never Advertised

Brown has never advertised, but her work on "Face the Nation," and public service radio and TV programs built her reputation to the point where she has been a consultant to the White House during a number of different presidencies.

Today she wears many professional "hats." She's radio/TV coordinator at Georgetown University, producer of "University Forum" which is sponsored by the Consortium of Universities of the Washington Metropolitan Area, voice coach and diction teacher to Voice of America broadcasters, chief of makeup at CBS, Washington, and last, but definitely not least, media consultant to national candidates, government officials, and public speakers.

Politics has no part in Brown's makeups or consultations. "I work with both parties — always through the client's media consultant. I have nothing to do with the rhetoric of the speeches."

"To many people, a job like mine sounds glamorous, but in reality there's a certain amount of hardship in the long hours and travel. Many days are like this: When working with a Mississippi candidate, I was up at 4:30 a.m. to be on film location at 6:00, stayed there working with the crew until 3 p.m., then dashed off to drive 150 miles to catch a flight home from the New Orleans airport. And in two days in North Carolina, I rode six different planes!"

Although it would be challenging for a newcomer to try to match Brown's remarkable reputation, there are certain qualities, characteristics, or background she thinks the person should have to be successful:

Imagination, Education, Flexibility

1) "Creative imagination and ingeniousness. Humility helps you to be sensitive to famous persons' personal dilemmas."

2) "A good education. Today there's a lot more competition than when I started. To help you compete successfully, you should take radio/TV production or journalism in college and, if you can, go on and get your master's. Also, important as theory is, you should try to work summers in a radio or TV studio for hands-on experience. Even though a producer never touches the teleprompter, the person should *know* how to make it work!"

3) "Above all, a willingness to be flexible. You'll be working with a wide variety of people. Some you may think should be made over completely, but consider their individual merits. My own philosophy is that naturalness is an important asset. As a consultant I must consider eyeglasses, hair, clothes, and TV setting as a 'picture frame' to best present the person's natural gifts. It's important to recognize pitfalls and eliminate them early on."

"I love to see a potential broadcaster make it on the air . . . to see an uncertain public servant rise to his or her full potential as an elected national official. With results like these to continue inspiring one, what else can I say about a job like this except 'I love it!' "

ARCH LUSTBERG:
Actor, Professor, Author

Communications expert **Arch Lustberg** says that his entry into this field was not quite like a bolt of lighting. "It was a natural evolution from being a teacher of drama based on a series of things that have happened."

The events encompass many fields: actor, professor of speech and drama at Catholic University for ten years, author of *Testifying with Impact* and the recently published *Winning at Confrontation*, producer of the Tony Award-nominated Broadway musical, *Don't Bother Me, I Can't Cope*, business experience, and speech coach-consultant for members of Congress, the Cabinet, and TV network and news people.

Today he applies this varied background as Director of Media Education at the U.S. Chamber of Commerce, where he is both teacher and administrator, and is responsible for the Communicator Workshops® held throughout the country.

A Communications "Trainer"

Because of increasing interest in public communication, more and more people are turning to good professional trainers who work with them individually. Lustberg is concerned that some people are more *teachers* than trainers. "Communication skills are as important as informational skills. A good trainer can train in any subject he or she knows well IF the person can be enthusiastic about the subject! For example, I might not take on individual retirement accounts, but could train in speed reading because I consider it fascinating. Someone else might choose the reverse."

Given the magnetic charge of excitement, someone with teaching experience can be a very likely candidate for what Lustberg describes as "the field of tomorrow." He not only suggests training as a good way for a teacher to make more money, but likes the satisfaction of giving clients confidence in their public appearances by knowing that they are at their best — that they are not imitating others, but being themselves.

PATRICIA MARKUN AND SHERRY WACKOWSKI:
Speechwriters
Behind the Scenes

No discussion of public-image people would be complete without mentioning those who frequently work behind the scenes, tackle a variety of subjects in a competent manner, try to anticipate problems, and create memorable, persuasive words: the Speechwriters.

It's only in recent years that there has been an increase of women in this field. Titles are as varied as those of the two women who founded the Washington Speechwriters Roundtable (an informal group of men and women who are on the staffs of or freelance for associations, government agencies, politicians, or corporations). **Patricia Markun** is Manager of Corporate Speaker Activities at the Federal Home Loan Mortage Corporation; **Sherry Wackowski** is Assistant Director of Editorial Services at the American Bankers Association. Both are speechwriters, and very good ones.

Markun says that speechwriting has traditionally been considered a "man's profession" because of the "close shadow" aspect of such relationships as speechwriter **Theodore Sorensen's** and **President Kennedy**. It was just a little more than 10 years ago that the media focused national attention on a woman, **Cynthia Rosenwald**, who wrote speeches for **Spiro Agnew**. However, the words "Baltimore housewife" followed her name so frequently that they seemed almost like a hyphenated addition!

Taking On Someone Else's Personality

Today there is far greater acceptance of women in the field, but whether the writer is a man or woman, Markun believes that there are certain qualities they should have: a fluency in writing AND writing for the ear, an ability to be able to write anonymously and to take on the personality of someone else, to be a good enough researcher to become knowledgeable about the subjects in which the client is a specialist without actually being an economist or financial expert. The result should be that one can adopt the lingo of another person or profession and do the kind of job that is creditable as well as credible. Markun also recomends a background of newspaper training or a journalism degree.

The Prime P.R. Tool

Wackowski underscores Markun's comments about good writing ability and the need for flexibility, but adds these recommendations for rookie speechwriters:

"Good interpersonal skills are very important. About 50 percent of having your speech accepted successfully may be the discussions you'll have with your client or other high-ranking executives. That's why public relations *plus* general writing experience is such a helpful background. Speeches are a prime P.R. tool.

"One also should accept the idea of being a 'ghost writer' . . . knowing that the compliments will all go to the *presenter* of the speech. However, there are so many tradeoffs for this anonymity that all adds up to a career that's very worthwhile."

What You Can Do

1. Talk with a television makeup artist or camera person to see how television lighting affects the subject.

2. Try to get "hands-on" television experience as well as a good theoretical education.

3. Be fully aware of the "unspoken signals" of communication . . . particularly the ones which turn an audience off (as a starter, you can make a list of the things that turn *you* off in the way a speaker gestures, dresses, has speech idiosyncrasies or mannerisms.)

4. Whenever there is a speech to be given (whether you're the presenter or writing it for someone else) read it aloud first to make sure it really is written for the *ear.*

5. Develop your interpersonal skills.

Conclusion

Now that you've read what the experts have to tell you I hope you'll be inspired to hang out your shingle and join their ranks. As you can tell from the experiences of those already in this field, being an image consultant can be a very colorful and exciting job. In the years ahead, the opportunities are likely to expand into areas we haven't even dreamed about at present.

Good Luck!

Reading You May Find Helpful

These books are a sampling of many available on subjects related to the fields of image and business. Most should be available in local book stores or libraries. If you have any difficulty in locating them, write to the publisher for additional information.

Albers, Josef, *Interaction of Color,* Also paperback, Yale University Press, Revised 1975.

Auerbach, Sylvia, *A Woman's Book of Money: A Guide to Financial Independence,* paperback, Doubleday, 1976.

Bates, Jefferson D., *Writing with Precision,* Hardcover or Paperback, Acropolis, 1978, revised 1981; *Dictating Effectively,* Also paperback, Acropolis, 1981.

Birren, Faber, *Color and Human Response,* Van Nos Reinhold, 1978; *Color Psychology and Color Therapy,* paperback, Citadel Press, 1978.

Cho, Emily, and Glover, Linda. *Looking Terrific: Express Yourself Through the Language of Clothing,* Putnam, 1978. Also paperback, Ballantine, 1979.

Cho, Emily, and Lueders, Hermine. *Looking, Working, Living Terrific 24 Hours a Day,* Putnam, 1982.

Eiseman, Leatrice. *Alive with Color,* Acropolis, 1983.

Feingold, Dr. S. Norman, and Perlman, Dr. Leonard G. *Making It On Your Own,* Also paperback, Acropolis, 1981.

Fendel, Alyson. *Waiting in Style,* Also paperback, Acropolis, 1983.

Fletcher, Leon. *How to Speak like a Pro,* paperback, Ballantine, 1983.

Gray, James G., Jr. *The Winning Image,* AMACOM (American Management Association), 1982.

Head, Edith. *How to Dress for Success,* Random House, 1967.

Hix, Charles. *Looking Good: A Guide for Men*, Hawthorne, 1977. Paperback, Wallaby Pocket Book, 1978. *Dressing Right. A Guide For Men*, with Burdine, Brian; St. Martin, 1978. Paperback, 1979.

Holtz, Herman. *How to Succeed as an Independent Consultant*, John Wiley & Sons, 1983.

Jackson, Carole. *Color Me Beautiful*, Acropolis, 1980. Paperback, Ballantine, 1981.

Jewell, Diana Lewis and Fiedorek, Mary B. *Executive Style. Looking It, Living It*, New Century Publishing Inc., 1983.

Kefgen, Mary and Pouchie-Specht, Phyllis. *Individuality in Clothing Selection and Dress*, Macmillan (3rd edition, 1981).

Lasser, J. *How to Run a Small Business*, McGraw-Hill, 1974.

Lustberg, Arch. *Testifying with Impact*, 1982; *Winning at Confrontation*, 1983, paperbacks, Association Division, U.S. Chamber of Commerce.

McCaslin, Barbara S. and McNamara, Patricia. *Be Your Own Boss: A Woman's Guide to Planning and Running Her Business*, Prentice-Hall, 1980.

McGill, Leonard. *Stylewise — A Man's Guide to Looking Good for Less*, Putnam, 1983.

McJimsey, Harriet T. *Art and Fashion in Clothing Selection*, Iowa State University Press, 1973. (1st edition, 1963).

Mitchell, Charlene and Burdick, Thomas. *The Extra Edge: Success Strategies for Women*, Acropolis, 1983.

Molloy, John T. *Dress for Success*, David McKay Inc., 1975. paperback, Warner Books, 1976. *The Woman's Dress for Success Book*, Follett Publishing Company, 1977. Paperback, Warner Books, 1978.

Morton, Grace Margaret. *The Arts of Costume and Personal Appearance*, John Wiley & Sons, (3rd edition, 1966 — original copyright, 1943).

Naisbitt, John. *Megatrends: Ten New Directions Transforming Our Lives*, Warner Books, 1982.

Olds, Ruthanne. *Big & Beautiful*, Acropolis, 1982 (Paperback title: *Stop Dieting, Start Living . . . the Big & Beautiful Way*, Acropolis, 1983.)

Sarnoff, Dorothy. *Make the Most of Your Best*, Doubleday, 1981. Paperback, Holt, Rinehart, Winston, 1983.

Spears, Charleszine. *How to Wear Color With Emphasis on Dark Skins*, Burgess Publishing Company, 1973-74.

Suzanne. *Color: The Essence of You*, Celestial Press, 1980.

Thompson, Jacqueline. *Image Impact*, paperback, Ace Books, 1982.

Wallach, Janet. *Working Wardrobe*, Acropolis, 1981. Paperback, Warner Books, 1982.

Winston, Stephanie. *Getting Organized*, W.W. Norton & Company, 1978. Paperback, Warner Books, 1979.

Also Available:

Directory of Personal Image Consultants, and "A Career in Personal Image Consulting."

Write to: Jacqueline Thompson,
Editorial Services, 96 State St.,
Brooklyn Heights, NY 11201

Addresses Of Organizations Of Interest To The Image Consultant:

American Society of Fashion and Image Consultants
1903 Kirby Road
McLean, Virginia 22101
(703) 442-9411

The International Institute of Professional Image Consultants
Colortone Building
2400 17th Street N.W.
Washington, D.C. 20009
(202) 387-6805

Footnotes

[1] Excerpts reprinted by permission from April 1983 issue of *Association Management Magazine.* Copyright 1983, by the American Society of Association Executives.

[2] "Color This Consulting Business Successful," *Entrepreneur,* October, 1982.

[3] Dr. S. Norman Feingold and Dr. Leonard G. Perlman, *Making it On Your Own,* Acropolis Books, 1981.

[4] From *Contemporary Authors,* vol 102, edited by Frances C. Locher (copyright © 1981 by Gale Research Company) Reprinted by permission of publisher. Gale, 1981, p. 271.

Consultant Contacts

Ms. Verdale Benjamin, President
Total Image Associates
P. O. Box 8242
Wichita, Kansas 67208

Ms. Lillian Brown
1003 Gelston Circle
McLean, Virginia 22102

Ms. Emily Cho
New Image
663 Fifth Avenue
New York, N.Y. 10021

Ms. Karen Davis
Color Concepts
5759 Heritage Hill Drive
Alexandria, Virginia 22310

Molloy "Dress for Success" Inc.
P. O. Box 526
Wash. Bridge Station
New York, N.Y. 10033

Ms. Leatrice Eiseman
18653 Ventura Boulevard Ste. 339
Tarzana, California 91356

Ms. Victoria Eubanks
Executive Director for the
Washington, D.C. area
Beauty For All Seasons
6401 Old Dominion Drive
McLean, Virginia 22101

Dr. S. Norman Feingold
President, National Career & Counseling
Services
1522 K Street, N.W. Ste. 336
Washington, D.C. 20005

Ms. Mary B. Fiedorek
c/o New Century Publishers, Inc.
220 Old Brunswick Rd.
Pisctaway, N.J. 08854

James G. Gray, Jr.
Media Impact
7510 Old Chester Rd.
Bethesda, Md. 20817

Ms. Cindy Harsley
"Persnickety"
1926 Newton Street N. E.
Washington, D.C. 20024

Mr. Lou Hampton, President
Hampton Communications Strategies
4200 Wisconsin Avenue, N.W. Ste. 106
Washington, D.C. 20016

Mr. Peter D. Hannaford
Chairman of the Board
The Hannaford Company, Inc.
444 South Flower Street Ste. 2620
Los Angeles, California 90017

Ms. Carole Jackson, Chairman of the Board
Color Me Beautiful International Headquarters
6817 Tennyson Drive
McLean, Virginia 22101

Ms. Harriet Kassman, owner
Harriet Kassman Inc.
4400 Jennifer Street, N.W.
Washington, D.C. 20016

Ms. Gerry Kendall
Fashion Consultant
Garfinckel's
14th and F Streets, N.W.
Washington, D.C. 20004

Mr. Arch Lustberg
Director of Media Education
U. S. Chamber of Commerce
1615 H Street, N.W.
Washington, D.C. 20062

Ms. Patricia Markun
Federal Home Loan Mortgage Corp.
1776 G Street, N.W.
Washington, D.C. 20006

Ms. Clare Miller
the five faces of woman
40001 McClary Ste. 2
Plano, Texas 75075

Ms. Helen Moody
6505 14th Street, N.W.
Washington, D.C. 20012

Ms. Ruthanne Olds
Image Communications Co.
P. O. Box 21399
Concord, California 94521

Ms. Mary Pennisi
The Color Studio
2880 Promenade Center
Richardson, Texas 75080

Ms. Doris Pooser
(Color Me Beautiful — *see listing for Carole Jackson*)

Dr. Deanna J. Radeloff, President
Deanna Radeloff & Associates Inc.
P. O. Box 520
Perrysburg, Ohio 43551

Ms. Lynda Rosenberg
Executive Wardrobe Consultants
1601 18th Street, N.W. Ste. 510
Washington, D.C. 20009

Ms. Holly Sallade
Color My Image, Ltd.
5105-I Backlick Road
Annandale, Virginia 22003

Ms. Nancy Ames Thompson
Image Awareness
4201 Cathedral Avenue, N.W.
Washington, D.C. 20016

Mrs. Glendys Tinkle
(Beauty For All Seasons — *see listing for Victoria Eubanks*)

Ms. Janet Wallach
c/o Acropolis Books, Ltd.
2400 17th Street, N.W.
Washington, D.C. 20009

Ms. Sherry Wackowski
300 Third Street, N. E.
Washington, D.C. 20002

Ms. Brenda York
York & Associates
1903 Kirby Road
McLean, Virginia 22101

Also corporate headquarters for:

Avon Products
9 W. 57th Street
New York, N.Y. 10019

Mary Kay Cosmetics, Inc.
Director, Field Support Services
8787 Stemmons Freeway
Dallas, Texas 75247

Among The Leading Color Systems

ALIVE WITH COLOR
18653 Ventura Boulevard Ste. 339
Tarzana, CA 91356

BEAUTICARE & COLOR™ By BeautiControl
Denise Turnage
2101 Midway
Carrollton, TX 75006
(214-458-0601)

BEAUTY FOR ALL SEASONS
Ms. Verla Ball, Vice President
P.O. Box 309
Idaho Falls, ID 83402

COLOR 1 ASSOCIATES, INC.
3176 Pullman Street Ste. 122
Costa Mesa, CA 92626

COLOR CONCEPT 7
Deanna Radeloff & Associates, Inc.
P.O. Box 520
Perrysburg, OH 43551

COLOR ME BEAUTIFUL, INC.
6817 Tennyson Drive
McLean, VA 22101

Also, for more information about the Fashion Academy program:

FASHION ACADEMY
2850 Mesa Verde Drive East
Costa Mesa, CA 92626

U.S. Small Business Administration Field Offices

Regional Offices

Region I

Regional Office
Small Business Administration
60 Battery March, 10th floor
Boston, Massachusetts 02110

Region II

Regional Office
Small Business Administration
26 Federal Plaza, Room 29–118
New York, New York 10007

Region III

Regional Office
Small Business Administration
231 St. Asaphs Road
1 Bala Cynwyd Plaza, Suite 646 West Lobby
Bala Cynwyd, Pennsylvania 19004

Region IV

Regional Office
Small Business Administration
1375 Peachtree Street, N.E.
Atlanta, Georgia 30309

Region V

Regional Office
Small Business Administration
Federal Building
219 South Dearborn Street, Room 838
Chicago, Illinois 60604

Region VI

Regional Office
Small Business Administration
1720 Regal Row
Regal Park Office Building, Room 230
Dallas, Texas 75235

Region VII

Regional Office
Small Business Administration
911 Walnut Street, 23rd floor
Kansas City, Missouri 64106

Region VIII

Regional Office
Small Business Administration
Executive Tower Building
1405 Curtis Street, 22nd floor
Denver, Colorado 80202

Region IX

Regional Office
Small Business Administration
450 Golden Gate Avenue
Box 36044
San Francisco, California 94102

Region X

Regional Office
Small Business Administration
710 2nd Avenue, 5th floor
Dexter Horton Building
Seattle, Washington 98104

District Offices

Region I

District Office
Small Business Administration
Federal Building
40 Western Avenue, Room 512
Augusta, Maine 04330

District Office
Small Business Administration
Federal Building
87 State Street, Room 204
P.O. Box 605
Montpelier, Vermont 05602

District Office
Small Business Administration
55 Pleasant Street, Room 213
Concord, New Hampshire 03301

District Office
Small Business Administration
150 Causeway Street, 10th floor
Boston, Massachusetts 02114

District Office
Small Business Administration
One Financial Plaza
Hartford, Connecticut 06103

District Office
Small Business Administration
57 Eddy Street, 7th floor
Providence, Rhode Island 02903

Region II

District Office
Small Business Administration
26 Federal Plaza, Room 3100
New York, New York 10007

District Office
Small Business Administration
Federal Building, Room 1071
100 South Clinton Street
Syracuse, New York   13260

District Office
Small Business Administration
970 Broad Street, Room 1635
Newark, New Jersey   07102

District Office
Small Business Administration
Chardon and Bolivia Streets
P.O. Box 1915
Hato Rey, Puerto Rico   00919

Region III

District Office
Small Business Administration
231 St. Asaphs Road
1 Bala Cynwyd Plaza, Suite 400 East Lobby
Bala Cynwyd, Pennsylvania   19004

District Office
Small Business Administration
Federal Building
1000 Liberty Avenue, Room 1401
Pittsburgh, Pennsylvania   15222

District Office
Small Business Administration
Oxford Building
8600 LaSalle Road, Room 630
Towson, Maryland   21204

District Office
Small Business Administration
109 North 3rd Street, Room 301
Lowndes Bank Building
Clarksburg, West Virginia   26301

District Office
Small Business Administration
1030 15th Street N.W., Suite 250
Washington, D.C.   20417

District Office
Small Business Administration
Federal Building
400 North 8th Street, Room 3015
Box 10126
Richmond, Virginia   23240

Region IV

District Office
Small Business Administration
Federal Building, 600 Federal Place, Room 188
Louisville, Kentucky   40202

District Office
Small Business Administration
404 James Robertson Parkway, Suite 1012
Nashville, Tennessee   37219

District Office
Small Business Administration
Providence Capitol Building, Suite 690
200 E. Pascagoula Street
Jackson, Mississippi   39201

District Office
Small Business Administration
908 South 20th Street, Room 202
Birmingham, Alabama   35205

District Office
Small Business Administration
Federal Building
400 West Bay Street, Room 261
P.O. Box 35067
Jacksonville, Florida   32202

District Office
Small Business Administration
2222 Ponce De Leon Blvd., 5th floor
Coral Gables, Florida   33134

District Office
Small Business Administration
1720 Peachtree Street, N.W., 6th floor
Atlanta, Georgia   30309

District Office
Small Business Administration
230 S. Tryon Street, Suite 700
Charlotte, North Carolina   28202

District Office
Small Business Administration
1801 Assembly Street, Room 131
Columbia, South Carolina   29201

Region V

District Office
Small Business Administration
1240 East 9th Street, Room 317
Cleveland, Ohio   44199

District Office
Small Business Administration
Federal Building, U.S. Courthouse
85 Marconi Boulevard
Columbus, Ohio   43215

District Office
Small Business Administration
575 North Pennsylvania Street, Room 552
New Federal Building
Indianapolis, Indiana   46204

District Office
Small Business Administration
Federal Building
219 South Dearborn Street, Room 437
Chicago, Illinois   60604

District Office
Small Business Administration
477 Michigan Avenue
McNamara Building
Detroit, Michigan   48226

District Office
Small Business Administration
212 East Washington Avenue, 2nd floor
Madison, Wisconsin   53703

District Office
Small Business Administration
12 South 6th Street
Plymouth Building
Minneapolis, Minnesota   55402

Region VI

District Office
Small Business Administration
1001 Howard Avenue
Plaza Tower, 17th floor
New Orleans, Louisiana   70113

District Office
Small Business Administration
611 Gaines Street, Suite 900
Little Rock, Arkansas   72201

District Office
Small Business Administration
Federal Building
200 N.W. 5th Street, Suite 670
Oklahoma City, Oklahoma   73102

Image
Consulting

District Office
Small Business Administration
5000 Marble Avenue, N.E.
Patio Plaza Building, Room 320
Albuquerque, New Mexico 87110

District Office
Small Business Administration
1100 Commerce Street, Room 3C36
Dallas, Texas 75242

District Office
Small Business Administration
One Allen Center
500 Dallas Street
Houston, Texas 77002

District Office
Small Business Administration
222 East Van Buren Street
P.O. Box 9253
Harlington, Texas 78550

District Office
Small Business Administration
727 E. Durango, Room A–513
Federal Building
San Antonio, Texas 78206

Region VII

District Office
Small Business Administration
1150 Grande Avenue, 5th floor
Kansas City, Missouri 64106

District Office
Small Business Administration
Mercantile Tower, Suite 2500
One Mercantile Center
St. Louis, Missouri 63101

District Office
Small Business Administration
New Federal Building
210 Walnut Street, Room 749
Des Moines, Iowa 50309

District Office
Small Business Administration
19th & Farnum Street
Empire State Building, 2nd Floor
Omaha, Nebraska 68102

District Office
Small Business Administration
110 East Waterman Street
Main Place Building
Wichita, Kansas 67202

Region VIII

District Office
Small Business Administration
721 19th Street
Denver, Colorado 80202

District Office
Small Business Administration
Federal Building
125 South State Street, Room 2237
Salt Lake City, Utah 84138

District Office
Small Business Administration
Federal Building, Room 4001
100 East B Street
P.O. Box 2839
Casper, Wyoming 82602

District Office
Small Business Administration
Federal Office Building, Room 528
301 South Park, Drawer 10054
Helena, Montana 59601

District Office
Small Business Administration
Federal Building
657 2nd Avenue, North, Room 218
P.O. Box 3086
Fargo, North Dakota 58102

District Office
Small Business Administration
National Bank Building
8th & Main Avenue, Room 402
Sioux Falls, South Dakota 57102

Region IX

District Office
Small Business Administration
3030 North Central Avenue, Suite 1201
Phoenix, Arizona 85012

District Office
Small Business Administration
301 E. Stewart
Box 7527, Downtown Station
Las Vegas, Nevada 89101

District Office
Small Business Administration
350 S. Figueroa Street, 6th floor
Los Angeles, California 90071

District Office
Small Business Administration
880 Front Street
Federal U.S. Building, Room 4–S–38
San Diego, California 92188

District Office
Small Business Administration
211 Main Street, 4th floor
San Francisco, California 94105

District Office
Small Business Administration
300 Ala Moana
P.O. 50207
Honolulu, Hawaii 96850

Region X

District Office
Small Business Administration
1005 Main Street, 2nd floor
Continental Life Building
P.O. Box 2618
Boise, Idaho 83701

District Office
Small Business Administration
915 Second Avenue
Federal Building, Room 1744
Seattle, Washington 98174

District Office
Small Business Administration
1016 West 6th Avenue, Suite 200
Anchorage Legal Center
Anchorage, Alaska 99501

District Office
Small Business Administration
1220 S.W. Third Avenue
Federal Building
Portland, Oregon 97204

District Office
Small Business Administration
Court House Building, Room 651
P.O. Box 2167
Spokane, Washington 99210

Small Business
Administration

Index

Free!

Send for your complimentary copy of THE IMAGE TRENDSLETTER, a newsletter devoted to the latest trends in color, fashion, home interiors, imaging.

☐ Yes! Please send me a complimentary issue of THE IMAGE TRENDSLETTER.

☐ Yes! Send me your free catalog of books for Woman Business Executives.

Send information to...

NAME_____

ADDRESS_____

CITY_____STATE_____ZIP_____

Send information to my friend or colleague...

NAME_____

ADDRESS_____

CITY_____STATE_____ZIP_____

MAIL TO:

Jennifer Prost
Acropolis Books Ltd.
2400 17th St., N.W.
Washington, D.C. 20009